A Retreat With
Francis de Sales, Jane de Chantal and Aelred of Rievaulx

Befriending Each Other in God

Wendy M. Wright

ST. ANTHONY MESSENGER PRESS

Cincinnati, Ohio

Other titles in the A Retreat With... *Series:*

of the Merton Legacy Trust.

Excerpt from *The Courage for Truth: The Letters of Thomas Merton to Writers* by Thomas Merton, edited by Christine M. Bochen. Copyright ©1993 by the Merton Legacy Trust. Reprinted by permission of Farrar, Straus and Giroux, Inc.

Reprinted by permission of The Putnam Publishing Group from *Waiting for God* by Simone Weil. Copyright ©1951 by G.P. Putnam's Sons.

Excerpt from *The Four Loves* by C.S. Lewis, copyright ©1960 by Helen Joy Lewis, reprinted by permission of Harcourt Brace and Company.

Excerpt from *The Collected Works of St. Teresa of Avila*, Vol. I, trans. Kieran Kavanaugh and Otilio Rodriguez, copyright ©1976 by the Washington Province of Discalced Carmelites, ICS Publications, 2131 Lincoln Road, N.E., Washington, D.C. 20002. Reprinted by permission.

Excerpts from *Treatise on the Love of God* by Francis de Sales, trans. Rev. Henry Mackey, O.S.B., copyright ©1942 by the Newman Book Shop, reprinted by permission of TAN Books and Publications.

Excerpts from *On Spiritual Friendship* by Aelred of Rievaulx, Cistercian Fathers Series, Five, trans. Mary Eugenia Laker, copyright ©1974 by Cistercian Publications, Inc., reprinted by permission of Cistercian Publications.

Excerpts from *Introduction to the Devout Life* by St. Francis de Sales. Copyright ©1950 by Harper and Brothers. Used by permission of Doubleday, a division of Bantam Doubleday Dell Publishing Group, Inc.

Cover illustration by Steve Erspamer, S.M.
Cover and book design by Mary Alfieri
Electronic format and pagination by Sandra Digman

ISBN 0-86716-239-2

Copyright ©1996, Wendy M. Wright

Published by St. Anthony Messenger Press
Printed in the U.S.A.

Contents

Introducing A Retreat With...

Twenty years ago I made a weekend retreat at a Franciscan house on the coast of New Hampshire. The retreat director's opening talk was as lively as a long-range weather forecast. He told us how completely God loves each one of us—without benefit of lively anecdotes or fresh insights.

As the friar rambled on, my inner critic kept up a sotto voce commentary: "I've heard all this before." "Wish he'd say something new that I could chew on." "That poor man really doesn't have much to say." Ever hungry for manna yet untasted, I devalued any experience of hearing the same old thing.

After a good night's sleep, I awoke feeling as peaceful as a traveler who has at last arrived safely home. I walked across the room toward the closet. On the way I passed the sink with its small framed mirror on the wall above. Something caught my eye like an unexpected presence. I turned, saw the reflection in the mirror and said aloud, "No wonder he loves me!"

This involuntary affirmation stunned me. What or whom had I seen in the mirror? When I looked again, it was "just me," an ordinary person with a lower-than-average reservoir of self-esteem. But I knew that in the initial vision I had seen God-in-me breaking through like a sudden sunrise.

At that moment I knew what it meant to be made in the divine image. I understood right down to my size eleven feet what it meant to be loved exactly as I was.

Only later did I connect this revelation with one granted to the Trappist monk-writer Thomas Merton. As he reports in *Conjectures of a Guilty Bystander*, while standing all unsuspecting on a street corner one day, he was overwhelmed by the "joy of being...a member of a race in which God Himself became incarnate.... There is no way of telling people that they are all walking around shining like the sun."

As an absentminded homemaker may leave a wedding ring on the kitchen windowsill, so I have often mislaid this precious conviction. But I have never forgotten that particular retreat. It persuaded me that the Spirit rushes in where it will. Not even a boring director or a judgmental retreatant can withstand the "violent wind" that "fills the entire house" where we dwell in expectation (see Acts 2:2).

So why deny ourselves any opportunity to come aside awhile and rest on holy ground? Why not withdraw from the daily web that keeps us muddled and wound? Wordsworth's complaint is ours as well: "The world is too much with us." There is no flu shot to protect us from infection by the skepticism of the media, the greed of commerce, the alienating influence of technology. We need retreats as the deer needs the running stream.

An Invitation

This book and its companions in the *A Retreat With...* series from St. Anthony Messenger Press are designed to meet that need. They are an invitation to choose as director some of the most powerful, appealing and wise mentors our faith tradition has to offer.

Our directors come from many countries, historical eras and schools of spirituality. At times they are teamed to sing in close harmony (for example, Francis de Sales, Jane de Chantal and Aelred of Rievaulx on spiritual friendship). Others are paired to kindle an illuminating fire from the friction of their differing views (such as Augustine of Hippo and Mary Magdalene on human sexuality). All have been chosen because, in their humanness and their holiness, they can help us grow in self-knowledge, discernment of God's will and maturity in the Spirit.

Inviting us into relationship with these saints and holy ones are inspired authors from today's world, women and men whose creative gifts open our windows to the Spirit's flow. As a motto for the authors of our series, we have borrowed the advice of Dom Frederick Dunne to the young Thomas Merton. Upon joining the Trappist monks, Merton wanted to sacrifice his writing activities lest they interfere with his contemplative vocation. Dom Frederick wisely advised, "Keep on writing books that make people love the spiritual life."

That is our motto. Our purpose is to foster (or strengthen) friendships between readers and retreat directors—friendships that feed the soul with wisdom, past and present. Like the scribe "trained for the kingdom of heaven," each author brings forth from his or her storeroom "what is new and what is old" (Matthew 13:52).

The Format

The pattern for each *A Retreat With...* remains the same; readers of one will be in familiar territory when they move on to the next. Each book is organized as a seven-session retreat that readers may adapt to their own schedules or to the needs of a group.

Day One begins with an anecdotal introduction called "Getting to Know Our Director(s)." Readers are given a telling glimpse of the guide(s) with whom they will be sharing the retreat experience. A second section, "Placing Our Director(s) in Context," will enable retreatants to see the guides in their own historical, geographical, cultural and spiritual settings.

Having made the human link between seeker and guide, the authors go on to "Introducing Our Retreat Theme." This section clarifies how the guide(s) are especially suited to explore the theme and how the retreatant's spirituality can be nourished by it.

After an original "Opening Prayer" to breathe life into the day's reflection, the author, speaking with and through the mentor(s), will begin to spin out the theme. While focusing on the guide(s)' own words and experience, the author may also draw on Scripture, tradition, literature, art, music, psychology or contemporary events to illuminate the path.

Each day's session is followed by reflection questions designed to challenge, affirm and guide the reader in integrating the theme into daily life. A "Closing Prayer" brings the session full circle and provides a spark of inspiration for the reader to harbor until the next session.

Days Two through Six begin with "Coming Together in the Spirit" and follow a format similar to Day One. Day Seven weaves the entire retreat together, encourages a continuation of the mentoring relationship and concludes with "Deepening Your Acquaintance," an envoi to live the theme by God's grace, the director(s)' guidance and the retreatant's discernment. A closing section of Resources serves as a larder from which readers may draw enriching books, videos, cassettes and films.

We hope readers will experience at least one of those memorable "No wonder God loves me!" moments. And we hope that they will have "talked back" to the mentor(s), as good friends are wont to do.

A case in point: There was once a famous preacher who always drew a capacity crowd to the cathedral. Whenever he spoke, an eccentric old woman sat in the front pew directly beneath the pulpit. She took every opportunity to mumble complaints and contradictions— just loud enough for the preacher to catch the drift that he was not as wonderful as he was reputed to be. Others seated down front glowered at the woman and tried to shush her. But she went right on needling the preacher to her heart's content.

When the old woman died, the congregation was astounded at the depth and sincerity of the preacher's grief. Asked why he was so bereft, he responded, "Now who will help me to grow?"

All of our mentors in *A Retreat With...* are worthy guides. Yet none would seek retreatants who simply said, "Where you lead, I will follow. You're the expert." In truth, our directors provide only half the retreat's content. Readers themselves will generate the other half.

As general editor for the retreat series, I pray that readers will, by their questions, comments, doubts and decision-making, fertilize the seeds our mentors have planted.

And may the Spirit of God rush in to give the growth.

Gloria Hutchinson
Series Editor
Conversion of Saint Paul, 1995

Getting to Know Our Directors

We are about to embark on a week-long retreat whose
theme for reflection will be spiritual friendship. Our
guides will be three: Francis de Sales, charismatic bishop
of Geneva, Switzerland, who lived in Savoy (now France)
at the turn of the seventeenth century, and author of the
popular devotional guide, *Introduction to the Devout Life*;
his friend, Jane de Chantal, wife, mother, widow and
foundress of a religious community for women, the
Visitation of Holy Mary; and Aelred of Rievaulx,
twelfth-century prior of the Cistercian monastery of
Rievaulx in England and author of several spiritual
treatises, among them, *On Spiritual Friendship*.

The three persons upon whom we call to guide us in
our retreat are, in some respects, unlikely companions.
Two—Francis de Sales and Jane de Chantal—were quite
literally companions. But the third, Aelred of Rievaulx,
lived five centuries earlier. He may seem to be an
unlikely match for Francis and Jane because a vast
distance of time and space separates him from them. But
we, too, are separated from Francis and Jane by the chasm
of four centuries. Perhaps this makes us unlikely
companions for all three mentors!

I begin with the unlikeliness of this retreat not because
I think that people who lived long ago have nothing to
say to the twentieth century, but just the contrary: We can
glean much richness of insight and breadth of perspective
from the past. I begin with this caution, however, because
we tend to read spiritual writers, especially ancient

spiritual writers, as if the wisdom they share is always timeless, applicable in every circumstance for every person. We often forget that the men and women whom our tradition has memorialized as wise guides in the spiritual life were men and women rooted in a particular culture at a particular time, and their recorded spiritual verities were shaped by those particularities.

We forget, too, that our own spiritual lives—the ways we conceive of God and the process of cultivating intimacy with God—are likewise profoundly shaped by the moment and circumstances of our own lives. Although we go to God within the context of a spiritual tradition, that tradition is a living, growing one. The wisdom we appropriate from the past is not static or timeless, but dynamic and adapting itself to the present. There is then a certain "irrepeatability" to our present spiritual quest. We rightly live into and learn from the traditions of the past, but the dance of the Spirit's movement in the emerging moment cannot be predicted. It was this way always.

Our coming together with these three figures of the past, then, should be marked not only with respect and the eager receptivity so characteristic of spiritual hunger, but with a clear sense of the mutuality of our undertaking and a confidence in our own ability, as well as theirs, to discern the voice and will of God.

I turn now to our guides Francis, Jane and Aelred, who, although separated by the chasm of many years, will speak anew from these pages. I hope they will explore with us the dynamics and texture of the spiritual friendships so essential to becoming open to God.

Our seventeenth-century mentors, Francis de Sales and Jane de Chantal, were themselves spiritual friends. They met in March 1604 in Dijon, France, where Francis de Sales had come to deliver a series of Lenten sermons.

He was in his mid-thirties and gaining a reputation for effective preaching. He spoke, people said, "heart to heart," from a heart pulsing with the love of God in such a way that others' hearts were moved.

Francis' home was Annecy in the duchy of Savoy, just south of Geneva, the city where the militant Protestant citizenry forbade any Catholics to reside. Francis was, in fact, Bishop of Geneva, but because of the religious polarization that existed in Europe in the wake of the Protestant Reformation, residing in his diocese was impossible. His episcopal residence was instead situated in Annecy, a lakeside village high in the Alps. That was fine with Francis for he had been born just outside that very town.

Francis' parents were members of the Savoyard aristocracy, and Francis grew up in a comfort that was cultured, if provincial by the standards of the great cities of the day. He had been schooled in Paris by the Jesuits and in Padua, where he took degrees in law and theology. Entering the priesthood was his idea, certainly not his parents'. He soon became an auxiliary bishop and, upon the death of his predecessor, a bishop.

When he met baroness Jane de Chantal in 1604, she was a thirty-year-old widow with four young children. She had just returned to her native Dijon for the Lenten season to stay with her father, a prominent magistrate and civic leader in mercantile Dijon. At the time, she was in permanent residence at the country chateau of Monthelon where she and her children lived in difficult circumstances with her irascible father-in-law, the baron de Chantal. Also residing there was the baron's domineering housekeeper, with whom the old man had a questionable liaison. The baron's son, Jane's deceased husband, had been killed in a hunting accident a few years earlier, and the distraught young widow had been pressured to leave the baronial estates of Bourbilly and move to the provincial backwater of Monthelon with her father-in-law.

Jane attended the Dijon Lenten sermons with her father and thus began a relationship between her and Francis which progressed from a formal director-directee bond to an intense spiritual friendship lasting until Francis' death in 1622. During the 1604 Lenten season the two became acquainted, and Jane revealed to Francis her growing desire not to marry again but to give herself utterly to God. Her marriage had been happy, yet, despite pressure from relatives to remarry, the distraught widow was looking at her life in a new way. She desired to dedicate her life completely to the God she was discovering in her grief.

For a number of years, Jane, with Francis as her guide, waited, raised her children and nurtured herself in the spirit of prayer. In 1610 they founded together a unique religious community, the Visitation of Holy Mary, designed for women like Jane who felt drawn to a deep intimacy with God, yet whose circumstances (familial responsibilities, poor health, disabilities or age) prevented them from joining one of the austere, enclosed contemplative communities of the Church.

Much of Jane's later life was caught up in the labor of establishing and administering the pattern of life that characterized the Visitation. She also attended to the education of her children and arranged suitable marriages for them, worrying and fretting as any mother would over the choices they made as adolescents and young adults.

Francis' episcopal duties took him much farther afield. He was engaged in the administration of his diocese—preaching, teaching, overseeing the clergy and religious communities within the circle of his care. He was a zealous reformer of the Church, which in his day was very much in the throes of renewal and reform. Spurred by the Protestant challenge, the Catholic world underwent transformation—institutional, doctrinal and, most significantly, spiritual. Everywhere there was a zest for prayer, for spiritual reading, for service and sacrifice, for guidance in the ways of God. Francis met this challenge. He became the spiritual director for vast circles of people—some intimately through face-to-face conversations and letters, and others more remotely through his writings.

In 1608 Francis de Sales published the first edition of what was to become his most famous book, the *Introduction to the Devout Life,* which remains a classic today. The *Introduction* was based on his letters to a young Savoyard woman who had moved with her husband into courtly circles.

Francis' letters guided her in cultivating a life of intentional devotion amid the decadence and luxury of seventeenth-century aristocratic life. Francis thought of this young woman and all to whom he wrote as friends in the spirit—*Philotheas,* or lovers of God. Their friendship was rooted in their mutual spiritual quest. Both Francis and Jane were in contact with numerous *Philotheas,* spiritual seekers hungry for a taste of God's goodness and deepened presence in their lives.

Jane counseled and wrote primarily for the sisters of her religious community, the Visitation, but she was consulted by others, too. We know of these spiritual relationships as well as of Francis' and Jane's own relationship chiefly through their letters. The cultivation and nurturance of such God-centered friendships was, in their minds, central to authentic spiritual life.

Our third retreat guide, Aelred of Rievaulx, likewise considered friendship to be central to spiritual maturation. Aelred, like Francis and Jane, lived in a period of intense spiritual and ecclesial renewal and political turmoil. The twelfth century, the bulk of which Aelred's life spanned, was a lively one both in the history of the Church and in Aelred's native Britain. The wide-reaching ecclesial reforms of Pope Gregory, initiated in the mid-eleventh century, were being implemented, extending their sway into the British Isles. The political and cultural climate of those isles was powerfully conditioned by the Norman Conquest of 1066 and the resultant tensions and amalgams of power between Norman conquerors and the vanquished Anglo-Saxons.

Like others of his generation, Aelred, whose given name was Ethelred, had adapted his Anglo-Saxon nomenclature to the tastes of the new Norman rulers. His father was Eilaf Junior, a priest of Hexham, a town in the north of England. Father and son belonged to a long line of priests who for generations had passed on their religious duties along with their patrimony. In Aelred's day, this practice was coming to an end, since the Gregorian reforms issuing from Rome contained the prescription of mandatory celibacy for the clergy.

Aelred thus found himself faced with making other choices for his life than had his father. As an adolescent Aelred was sent north to the court of King David of the Scots in order to receive further education and to establish the ties necessary to exercise power and responsibility. He was reared with other young men his age, chiefly David's son, Henry, and two stepsons, Simon and Waldef. At the court Aelred enjoyed great popularity and developed especially close affective ties with one of these fellow students, attaching himself in a manner that he later came to regard as excessive and inappropriate.

Despite his popularity and success, Aelred was

restless. He longed for something more. When on a diplomatic mission to York, he visited the Cistercian abbey of Rievaulx. That visit forever changed his life. On the second day of his stay he offered himself at the gates of Rievaulx to become a monk.

The Cistercians were a newly reformed community of monks in the tradition of Benedictine monasticism who sought to live in the spirit of continual prayer and in the original primitive simplicity of the Rule of St. Benedict. There was enormous vitality in the Cistercian reform, a vitality perhaps best exemplified by the founding group's most notable figure, Bernard of Clairvaux. History has inherited exquisite expressions of religious architecture and gems of mystical literature from the group's twelfth-century flowering. Aelred enjoyed great popularity in his new life, being chosen as representative to Rome, novice master and founder of the new monastery of Revesby in his first decade of professed life. He returned to Rievaulx to assume the position of abbot. There he was responsible for the administration of his own community, which numbered over six hundred, as well as the supervision of Rievaulx's daughter houses, which multiplied during his years of office.

Somehow, along with thousands of letters, the abbot managed to write about the spiritual life. He seems to have done this with the urging of Bernard of Clairvaux himself, who took note of the spiritual depth and literary gifts of the young abbot. Aelred's most famous work, *On Spiritual Friendship,* was started at the onset of his tenure as abbot at Rievaulx, but was not completed until a full twenty years had passed. He wrote *On Spiritual Friendship* with the concerns of his monastic brethren foremost in mind. It is composed in the classical literary form of a philosophical dialogue. Inspired by the reading of Cicero's treatise on friendship, Christian friends gather to debate and discuss the nature of such a relationship as it might be pursued in the context of a mutual commitment to the gospels.

Aelred's book seems to have been one of those undertakings of self-discovery with which so many authors are familiar. The author was, by his own and other's accounts, an affectionate and personable fellow. His genius for friendship had, however, led him into situations which "corrupted his soul." After entering the monastic life and finding himself in the company of his many brothers in Christ, he wonders how he can "draw up rules for [him]self for a chaste and holy love." The resultant exploration produced one of the most original and thought-provoking treatises to deal with the phenomenon of friendship in all Christian literature.

Placing Our Directors in Context

If you had access to a library that contained all the classic literary expressions of Christian spirituality written in the last twenty centuries and you could scan the countless pages, you would discover that there are enduring themes with which the authors of this literature concern themselves. Prayer, repentance, humility, silence and divine love are a few. The list could go on. But the theme of this retreat, spiritual friendship, is one with which relatively few classic authors have been concerned. Most of those who have written of the spiritual journey have conceptualized it as an essentially solitary undertaking, a drama whose principal characters are the soul and God. The individual soul may live in community—monastic or otherwise—but relationships within that community are not considered part of how, and especially not as a primary means by which, that soul goes to God.

There are a few authors, however, who have lived in historical eras when the significance of relationships in the spiritual life was acknowledged, when the cast of the drama was enlarged to include not only God and the soul but others, especially friends. Usually these eras were ones in which Christian humanism was a prominent intellectual and cultural current informing thought and action.

Both the twelfth and the dawn of the seventeenth centuries in Europe were such eras. They are both eras to which historians have affixed the name "renaissance." The term means rebirth and refers to a rebirth of interest in the classical heritage of Greece and Rome. Chief of the interests in the classical world was humankind itself—the human body, intellect, emotions, political and social life, communication, the artistic and literary enterprises. So, too, in the twelfth and sixteenth- to early seventeenth-century "renaissances," European thinkers found themselves fascinated with the beauty, glory and pathos of the human condition. Unlike their classical predecessors, however, their fascination with humankind was situated within the framework of Christian revelation. Humanity was the focus, but it was a humanity created in the image and likeness of God. And humanity's original lost dignity had been redeemed through God's becoming human in Jesus the Christ.

So Aelred in the twelfth and Jane and Francis at the turn of the seventeenth century were steeped in the ethos of Christian humanism. When they wrote of the spiritual life, they turned first to the human experience of God among us. They explored human capacity as it enabled people to realize their innate Godwardness. They focused on the arts and acts of being human as the medium through which divine presence is mediated. They knew that people go home together to God. They thus concerned themselves with the relationships among people that best ease that mutual homecoming.

The twelfth and early seventeenth centuries were also eras in the Church's life when renewal and reform kept things lively and stirred up. The Church, like any human institution—political, economic or cultural—constantly changes. Each generation must internalize the faith anew. Each generation searches for authenticity in its own way. But there is also a more overarching dynamic of change which spans generations and produces periods of intense religious creativity. In the process, old patterns of religiosity break up. New patterns emerge. It is very alive.

The twelfth century was a time of economic and cultural vitality in most of Europe. The continent and the British Isles were by this time Christianized so that all people shared a certain unity and identity. The papacy under Gregory VII had instituted a series of reforms that invigorated the episcopate, eliminated the inappropriate sale of Church offices and property, and instituted moral sanctions for the clergy. Monastic life was flourishing.

The previous century had seen the creation of several new hermit orders whose austere commitment to the life of prayer inspired many. The twelfth century saw the reform of communal monastic life. The Benedictine rule had governed most monasteries for centuries, but observance had been adapted to the needs of increasingly wealthy and organizationally complex monasteries that had come to function as economic and political powers in feudal Europe.

Under the leadership of men like Bernard of Clairvaux, the primitive simplicity of Benedictine life was restored. The Cistercian order grew out of this restoration. Founding their houses in secluded areas, the

Cistercian monks lived austerely, alternating their time with manual labor and prayer. Their prayer was primarily (but not exclusively) communal. The community gathered at appointed times each day to pray the Divine Office. In solemn chanting, the monks acknowledged divine love, sang psalms and immersed themselves in Scripture, thus creating an atmosphere of continued and deepening recollection. Those who were drawn to the Cistercians, like Aelred of Rievaulx in the twelfth century and Thomas Merton in the twentieth, were men and women who took the spiritual life with utmost seriousness. They committed themselves to a deeper intimacy with the divine life itself.

At the core of Cistercian life was a spirituality shaped by the monastic life-style, yet deeply imbued with the humanistic optimism of the age. The Cistercian monk considered him or herself to be participating in the Christ life by embracing an ascetic martyrdom—by dying to the "self" that was formed by the greed, luxury, self-aggrandizement and lust for power inherent in the "world" and rising to a new self in Christ characterized by charity, humility and purity of heart. This transformation was to be realized in a self-contained, stable community remote from ordinary society—the monastery—where this deep transformation could be cultivated.

Cistercian life made much of the communal aspect of this transformative venture. Community members went together to God. And Cistercian writers revealed themselves most fully when they prayed and wrote about the Incarnation, about God becoming human. This gift, they knew, was a gift of abiding love on the part of a God whose love for humankind was lavish. Such a loving gift must not only be acknowledged, it must be received. God must be "with us" in hearts humbly opened and made ready. And the gift must be lived: in the loving actions and relationships that we cultivate between ourselves and in the loving, affective relationships we establish with God. Thus the language of love—of nuptial union, of lover seeking the beloved, of intimate friendship—is the favored language of Cistercian spirituality.

An intensification of spirituality and renewal of religious life was also a feature of the late sixteenth and early seventeenth centuries. But by then Christians were experimenting with institutional forms other than monasticism. The mixed life of periodic withdrawal and active preaching was already practiced by the mendicant orders of Francis of Assisi and Dominic. Now, active service as much as contemplative withdrawal appealed to Christians eager to realize their religious aspirations. The Society of Jesus (the Jesuits) was only one of a cluster of groups formed for evangelization, teaching, charitable and missionary work on behalf of the Church of Rome. A group like the Visitation of Holy Mary founded by Jane de Chantal and Francis de Sales was part of this new experimentation, a seeking for new forms of life in which devout believers could channel their energies to the love and service of God.

All this ferment had, of course, been both spurred on and/or initiated by the challenge of the Christians who came to be called Protestant. The Reformation had rocked Christendom in the early sixteenth century, and the direct repercussions were felt for fully a hundred years. Within the churches loyal to Rome, renewal and reform moved quickly. The Council of Trent, called by the papacy at the close of the sixteenth century, had directed reform to educate the clergy, eliminate abuses of power and office, instruct the laity, and clarify doctrine.

This thorough institutional reform was sweeping through Europe during Francis' and Jane's lifetimes.

And, as in the twelfth century before, in the late sixteenth and early seventeenth centuries the effects of reform were felt, not only in Church life and policy but in the spiritual realm as well. Prayer, spiritual practices and devotional activity were popular now not only among the "professionally" religious but among the laity. Fresh translations of spiritual classics kept pace with publications of newly authored books on the spiritual life. Francis de Sales' *Introduction to the Devout Life* was among those publications.

The spirituality that the *Introduction* reflects is Salesian—the spiritual tradition created by Francis and Jane. Unlike Cistercian spirituality, with its assumption of a life of monastic withdrawal, Salesian spirituality is not linked to a specific life-style or "state in life." In this it reflects the diverse Church of the Counter-Reformation, with both its renewed affirmation of the monastic vocation and its heightened interest in the cultivation of a serious spiritual life by Christians in all walks of life.

At the heart of Salesian spirituality is the motto "Live Jesus." Jesus is to live in human hearts. The radical transformation of the worldly self is to take place interiorly and then manifest its fruits in whatever situation a person finds him or herself—as housewife, greengrocer, civil servant, aristocrat or peasant. Thus Jesus is hidden in the heart. The Jesus who is to live there is the gentle, humble Jesus portrayed in Matthew 11, the Jesus who is gentle and lowly of heart and invites all to take his yoke upon their shoulders. Thus much of Salesian spirituality emphasizes the cultivation of little, hidden virtues such as gentleness, simplicity, patience and loving kindness. These virtues are to be expressed where one finds oneself—in the midst of the busy life of family, friends, work and neighborhood.

Salesian spirituality emerged from a period much like

our own, a period when many people in all walks of life were searching for new and engaging ways to deepen their experience, a period in which a reader might eagerly seek out a series of retreat books as guides on the venture of the inward-outward journey into the mystery of God.

DAY ONE
A Universe of Love

Introducing Our Retreat Theme

In a short story by Flannery O'Connor entitled "Greenleaf," the wife of the title character is an odd, even eccentric, perhaps repelling, personality, as are many of O'Connor's characters. Mrs. Greenleaf is the wife of a shiftless tenant farmer. A lackadaisical housekeeper and abstracted mother, she is preoccupied with what she terms her "prayer healing." Every day she cuts all the morbid stories out of the newspaper—stories of death and disaster and mayhem—and takes them out into the woods, buries them in a hole and falls over them, moaning and groaning and imploring the name of Jesus, entreating him to "stab her in the heart." Mrs. Greenleaf is discovered at her bizarre intercessory ritual one day by the landowner's wife who shrinks back in startled horror, scolds the woman groveling in the dirt, and commands her to get up and go wash her children's clothes.[1]

Mrs. Greenleaf, in her curious way, is an appropriate figure with which to introduce our retreat. She confounds our sensibilities about the way things "should" happen. She startles us out of our habituated intimations about the order of the world. For one thing, she is a character whose priorities are different from most of ours. She truly puts God first. And she lives and operates out of the conviction that her prayer and flailing entreaties are intimately connected both to God and to other human beings.

For all her extreme expression, Mrs. Greenleaf is also a woman who takes seriously the idea that God really attends to the individual concerns of each human being. Her ritualistic clipping of newspaper articles and her invocation of Jesus bring particular persons, each with a name and a story, into the center of divine focus. And she knows that her willingness to take on another's pain, in union with Jesus whose redemptive love is also participatory, is the most important thing she can do. Mrs. Greenleaf shows us in her extraordinary way that God's love, our love for God and our love for one another are not simply sentimental ideas but profoundly transformative and interconnected realities. What she knows is that we are each called by name, not only by God but by one another, into the fullness and the hope for which our hearts long.

Most of us are fond of recalling that God calls us each "by name," that we are known as individuals, attended to and cherished in unique ways, and personally invited by God into a relationship of intimacy. Each of us—Maria, John, Robert, Carol and Jennifer—is called. But in fact our name is not singular. We are like our ancient forebears who were known by their parental or residential appellation. We are Jeanne of Chicago or Garrett from the United States. We are residents of our town, our county, our state, our nation, our part of the world. Calling our name also involves calling us by our full names—Maria Theresa Hernandez or John Frederick Jones. Names identify us as part of a family and part of a larger ethnic or cultural inheritance. Yet our name is, in fact, even fuller than this. Robert also answers to the name "Susan's husband" or "Dolores's brother." Carol is also "Ellen's daughter" or "Patrick's mother."

All this is to say that we are not simply isolated selves.
We are our contexts and our relationships. We are what
we belong to. And we are what we love. When God calls
us, God calls beings whose fullest identity is relational.

We cannot choose many of the relationships that make
us who we are. We are born of specific parents, we grow
up with unchosen siblings and in neighborhoods about
which we have not had our say. We do not have our
choice of sons and daughters. They come to us as they
are. We cannot always choose our colleagues at work or
all the members of the congregations to which we belong.
But we can choose some. This retreat is about those
relationships we choose that help to make us who we
want to be, relationships that help us deepen our
relationship with God. It is about friends—spiritual
friends.

Aelred of Rievaulx, Jane de Chantal and Francis de
Sales are our guides in this retreat. Each of them knew
that the journey into God, while profoundly personal, is
not private. Each of them knew spiritual friendships to be
loving relationships that enable us to grow in heart, mind
and wisdom to become better lovers of God.

As we enter this retreat with Aelred, Francis and Jane,
we might call to mind others as well, friends who have
been gift and grace to us over the years. Let each of them
enter the retreat with us, recalling the course of each
relationship, its particular quality, its unique place in our
spiritual odyssey. Let each distinct face, each name, each
story, animate our prayer throughout the retreat.

Opening Prayer

Gracious God,
you call us each by name.
But you do not simply call us alone,
you call us with each other.
You call us to you.
You stretch out your hand
and ask us to take it.

We stretch ours out in return
and find they are clasped
to sister, father, son,
neighbor, wife and friend.

How we hold each other
is how we hold you.
We have only one pair of hands,
not two.
The same pair of hands
does all the holding.

Take our outstretched,
intertwined hands.
Teach us truly to understand
that in the art of holding one another
we learn what it is to touch you.

RETREAT SESSION ONE

God calls us by name. We, too, call on God by name.
The names Christians have given to God are many and
varied. God is and has been creator, king, brother, father,
mother, lover, spirit, triune majesty, broken sacrificial

victim, tender manger-laid babe, infinite unfathomable abyss. The list is endless. There are names which Christians have returned to over and again, especially in worship, which seem to express most clearly the collective Christian sense of deity. There are names which individual lovers of God have found and do find resonant, names which reexpress the diversity of ways God comes and intertwines with our particular human lives. Perhaps God's greatest name of all is Love. Scripture tells us as much:

> My dear friends,
> let us love each other,
> since love is from God
> and everyone who loves is a child of God and knows
>   God.
> Whoever fails to love does not know God,
> because God is love. (1 John 4:7-8, NJB)[2]

That God is Love might seem commonplace. No doubt we have heard it proclaimed a thousand times. What we generally mean by this proclamation is that we conceive God to be loving, to express love toward us. But our three retreat directors have an insight into divine Love that goes even farther and is wonderfully enlivening.

Francis gives fullest expression to this insight in his *Treatise on the Love of God*, a rather long, fairly dense statement on "the history of the birth, progress, decay, operations, properties, advantages and excellences of divine love." In the *Treatise*, Francis, in good humanist fashion, begins with human experience, *our* experience of love. But undergirding the entire manuscript is his vision of a God who is, first and foremost, Love itself. It is the nature of Love, Francis insists, to overflow, to expand beyond itself in creativity and abundance. Thus creation itself is an act of divine love, love expressing its fullness. And creation remains sustained by Love. All that is has being because of Love. Sheer existence itself thus is suffused with Love. The nature of being, when truly grasped, *is* Love.

It is not simply that God who is Love at one time created us and the universe in which we find ourselves. *Our* very nature, as created beings, is essentially love. Our love and divine love are thus intimately connected. Francis uses wonderful metaphors to stress this truth.

> ...God is God of the human heart; and our understanding is never so filled with pleasure as in this thought of the divinity,...
>
> This pleasure, this confidence which [the human] heart naturally has in God can spring from no other root than the affinity there is between this divine goodness and [the] soul, a great but secret affinity, an affinity which each one knows but few understand, an affinity which cannot be denied nor yet be easily sounded. We are created to the image and likeness of God....
>
> But besides this affinity of likenesses, there is an incomparable correspondence between God and [hu]man[ity], for their reciprocal perfection: not that God can receive any perfection from [human beings] but because as [humanity] cannot be perfected but by the divine goodness, so the divine goodness can scarcely so well exercise its perfection outside itself, as upon our humanity: the one has great want and capacity to receive good, the other great abundance and inclination to bestow it.... The meeting then of abundance and indigence is most sweet and agreeable, and one could scarcely have said whether the abounding good have a greater contentment in spreading and communicating itself, or the failing and needy good in receiving and in drawing to

itself, until Our Saviour had told us that it *is more blessed to give than to receive*. Now where there is more blessedness there is more satisfaction, and therefore the divine goodness receives greater pleasure in giving than we in receiving.

Mothers' breasts are sometimes so full that they must offer them to some child, and though the child takes the breast with great avidity, the nurse offers it still more eagerly, the child pressed by its necessity, and the mother by her abundance.[3]

Clearly, Francis sees the love that flows between creator and creation as one in substance, yet different. Just as a parent loves differently from a child, although both parent and child are bound to one another through love, so divine and human love are one, yet different. Love gives of self because it is the nature of love to do so.

The picture that Francis paints for us is really quite breathtaking. Love, human and divine, is the fundamental principle of life. Hungry for the substance that will sustain us, we turn to God and suckle the Love that flows from the ample, divine breasts. As children of Love, we are not only nourished on love, we are love as well. Our deepest nature is to be discovered in fully realizing our capacity for love. Like God, we not only "have" love or behave in a loving manner, but when we are most authentically ourselves, we *are* love.

Our love, like God, longs to overflow, to create and ultimately return to the source of its being—God. Francis states it this way:

The end then of love is no other thing than the *union* of the lover and the thing loved....as love tends to union, even so union very often extends and augments love: for love makes us seek the society of the beloved, and this often nourishes and increases love; love causes a desire of nuptial union, and this union reciprocally preserves and increases love, so that in every sense it is true that love tends to union.[4]

Thus Francis paints for us a picture of a universe of love. Love that spills over from Creator to creation. Love that flows back from creature to Creator in generous, joyous return. For men and women, love of God is neither pious duty nor a denial of our humanity. To love God is to be fully human, fully alive. It is to activate our innate depths.

For Reflection

- *What is the name of God with which you have the deepest resonance? What is revealed about God and about yourself in this name?*

- *What is your past and present experience of God as Love?*

- *Explore the ways in which God's love has expressed itself in your life.*

- *Imagine yourself in a congregation to which Francis de Sales is preaching. How do you respond when he preaches that "God is the God of the human heart"? When he likens God to a nursing mother? When he uses marriage (nuptial) imagery to describe the relationship between human beings and God?*

- *Preach a sermon using your own metaphors for God's love. In a group, share your sermons.*

For Further Reflection and Discussion

It is not easy to try to say what I know I cannot say.
I do really have the feeling that you have all
understood and shared quite perfectly. That you
have seen something that I see to be most precious—
and most available too. The reality that is present to
us and in us: call it Being, call it Atman, call it
Pneuma...or Silence. And the simple fact that by
being attentive, by learning to listen (or recovering
the natural capacity to listen which cannot be
learned any more than breathing), we can find
ourself engulfed in such happiness that it cannot be
explained: the happiness of being at one with
everything in that hidden ground of Love for which
there can be no explanations.[5]—Thomas Merton

Closing Prayer

Gracious God,
yours is a universe of love.
Your love spills out in creation
and creation longs to love you
in return.

Teach us to reverence
all that is most human.
For what is most human
is created by and for the divine.

Notes

[1] Flannery O'Connor, "Greenleaf," in *The Complete Stories* (New York: Farrar, Straus and Giroux, 1971), p. 315.

[2] Scripture citations are taken from *The New Jerusalem Bible* (designated NJB) or the *New Revised Standard Version* (designated NRSV).

[3] Francis de Sales, *Treatise on the Love of God*, trans. the Rev. Henry Benedict Mackey, O.S.B. (Westminster, Md.: Newman Book Shop, 1942), pp. 54-55.

[4] Ibid., pp. 39, 40.

[5] "Letter to Amiya Chakravarty" in *The Hidden Ground of Love: The Letters of Thomas Merton on Religious Experience and Social Concerns*, ed. William H. Shannon (New York: Farrar, Straus, Giroux, 1985), p. 115.

Day Two
The Love of Friends

Coming Together in the Spirit

> This is my commandment:
> love one another,
> as I have loved you....
> You are my friends,
> if you do what I command you.
> I shall no longer call you servants,...
> I call you friends,...
> My command to you
> is to love one another. (John 15:12, 14-15, 17, NJB)

The Scriptures are love letters from God. If we sit with them and let them speak to us like messages from a beloved friend or lover, they come alive in a special way. We find ourselves savoring them, tasting them, touching them, turning them over and committing them to memory. During the day, even when we are not looking at our letters, they come to mind. Fragments and phrases, they find a home in our hearts.

Throughout this retreat, the daily session will begin with a fragment from one of God's love letters. Let it be that for you, carrying its consoling and challenging words into the retreat session.

Defining Our Thematic Content

We live in a universe of love. God, our loving creator, fashions us in the divine image. Thus we are most fully what we were intended to be when we, like God, actualize our capacity to love. We do that by loving God in return and by loving one another. Divine and human love are the two partners in the cosmic dance of creator and creation, two partners whose steps link infinity and finitude.

Among contemporary Christians few have documented their love for and dependence on spiritual friends as openly as Thomas Merton. The Cistercian monk and popular author had a great gift for friendships, many of which were crucial to his becoming what God intended him to be. As a young man Merton exhibited many of the traits that would later serve him in good stead. Passionate, gifted, possessed of a fierce humor, he was a born seeker.

But one wonders if he would have turned his gifts to God's service had it not been for the influence of friends, especially the friends he made at Columbia University, where Merton studied in the mid-1930's. He had arrived at the New York university by way of Cambridge in England and a chaotic year an acquaintance described as one of "beer, bewilderment and sorrow." His family decimated, his relationships awry, his spiritual longings unfocused and unhoused, the young Merton met Mark van Doren, a poet who taught English literature and who mentored him into a quest for the deeper realities of life; Bob Lax, a fellow student, possessed, as Merton said, of a natural, instinctiee spirituality, a kind of inborn direction to the living God; and Ed Rice, a Catholic compatriot.

Through these friends and the presence of friends found in books—principally the medieval philosopher

Etienne Gilson, the English poet William Blake and the novelist Aldous Huxley—Merton began to understand his innate, inchoate longings as Godward leanings and to shape them into the vessel that would finally become his life. Monastic commitment and the composition of many books on contemplation and the spiritual life followed. But it was the friendships that enabled Merton's true, God-directed life to be born.

Opening Prayer

> Loving God,
> you are the life of the universe.
> Your life is love.
> You ask us to love as we have been loved.
>
> Teach us to love one another
> with your mercy, your tenderness.
> Make our love as wide
> as the arms you stretched out
> to embrace the world.

RETREAT SESSION TWO

It is not uncommon to hear people say, when they want to underplay the importance of a relationship, "Oh, he (or she) is just a friend." "Friend" becomes a category for those people in our lives who are not spouses or lovers, not close relatives, not workplace associates and not neighbors. They don't count as significant others. They are "just friends."

Our retreat directors no doubt would shake their heads at such casual asides. Just friends? For all three mentors friendship was a unique and precious type of relationship that required attentiveness and care. In fact, they thought of friendship as a particular type of love. Aelred attempted a definition while conversing with his monastic brethren. We find his reflections recorded in *On Spiritual Friendship*.

> Friendship is mutual harmony in affairs human and divine.... I think the word *amicus* (friend) comes from the word *amor* (love), and *amicitia* (friendship) from *amicus*. For love is a certain "affection" of the rational soul whereby it seeks and eagerly strives after some object to possess it and enjoy it. Having attained its object through love, it enjoys it with a certain interior sweetness, embraces it and preserves it....
>
> Furthermore, a friend is called a guardian of love.... It is fitting that my friend be a guardian of our mutual love...[to] cure and endure such defects as he may observe...rejoice with his friend in his joys, and weep with him in his sorrows, and feel as his own all that his friend experiences...friendship...is that virtue by which spirits are bound by ties of love and sweetness, and out of many are made one....[1]

Aelred, following the thinking of the Roman philosopher Cicero, had concluded that there were varieties of love, related to one another, but different in significant ways. Love is a connecting energy, a force that draws and binds together, a power that makes disparate entities one. Human beings experience different sorts of love. We know romantic love, the passionate union of lover and beloved which seeks complete union. We also know familial love, the particular powerful ties that bind us as parent and child, brother and sister. We know as well a more universal, altruistic love, an empathic concern for our fellow human beings. And we know the love of friends.

Friendship is a unique love because, unlike other loves, it is by necessity mutual and equal. A lover can pine after a beloved and not have that love returned. Mothers and fathers do not love their children in the same way that daughters and sons love their parents. The universal love of humanity is hardly reciprocal. It may even be anonymous. But friendship requires mutuality and equality. Unless both partners in a friendship are invested in the relationship, it will cease to be. Unless both recognize each other as equal, the friendship cannot involve a true exchange and sharing of perspectives.

Friendship is that most delicate of loves that does not depend upon blood ties or the conjoining of lives. The love of friends is open-handed. It receives and gives love as a gift. Aelred can scarcely contain himself when he waxes eloquent on the joys of such a relationship where the friend is "another self."

> But what happiness, what security, what joy to have someone to whom you dare to speak on terms of equality as to another self; one to whom you need have no fear to confess your failings; one to whom you can unblushingly make known what progress you have made in the spiritual life; one to whom you can entrust all the secrets of your heart and before whom you can place all your plans! What, therefore, is more pleasant than so to unite to oneself the spirit of another and of two to form one, that no boasting is thereafter to be feared, no suspicion to be dreaded, no correction of one by the other to cause pain, no praise on the part of one to bring a charge of adulation from the other. "A

friend," says the Wise Man, "is the medicine of life."
Excellent, indeed, is that saying. For medicine is not
more powerful or more efficacious for our wounds
in all our temporal needs than the possession of a
friend who meets every misfortune joyfully, so that,
as the Apostle says, shoulder to shoulder, they bear
one another's burdens. Even more—each one carries
his own injuries even more lightly than that of his
friend. Friendship, therefore, heightens the joys of
prosperity and mitigates the sorrows of adversity by
dividing and sharing them. Hence, the best
medicine in life is a friend. Even the philosophers
took pleasure in the thought: not even water, nor the
sun, nor fire do we use in more instances than a
friend. In every action, in every pursuit, in certainty,
in doubt, in every event and fortune of whatever
sort, in private and in public, in every deliberation,
at home and abroad, everywhere friendship is
found to be appreciated, a friend a necessity, a
friend's service a thing of utility. "Wherefore,
friends," says Tullius, "though absent are present,
though poor are rich, though weak are strong,
and—what seems stranger still—though dead are
alive. And so it is that the rich prize friendship as
their glory, the exiles as their native land, the poor
as their wealth, the sick as their medicine, the dead
as their life, the healthy as their charm, the weak as
their strength and the strong as their prize. So great
are the distinction, memory, praise and affection
that accompany friends that their lives are adjudged
worthy of praise and their death rated as precious.
And, a thing even more excellent than all these
considerations, friendship is a stage bordering upon
that perfection which consists in the love and
knowledge of God, so that man from being a friend
of his fellowman becomes the friend of God,
according to the words of the Saviour in the Gospel:
"I will not now call you servants, but my friends."[2]

Love is not simply sentiment for our retreat directors. They draw upon a biblical understanding of love that is quite otherwise: "[L]ove is strong as Death,...Love no flood can quench, no torrents drown" (Song of Songs 8:6, 7, NJB). Nor is love only libido, the instinctual biological drive toward self-satisfaction, nor is it simply solidarity based on kinship. Love is the fabric of being itself.

Francis de Sales is quoted as saying that human beings do not have two hearts—one that loves God and one that loves neighbors—but only one heart that does all our loving. Love, with its intense dynamics of desire and its power to unite and bind, is given to unite persons with the creator from whom they come. It is also given so that we might be bound with one another and complete together that return to the divine source. Friendship is one of the ways we love one another and complete our journey home.

Our retreat directors took friendship very seriously, considering it a unique form of love with specific characteristics all its own. Our contemporary culture with its excessive mobility, its busyness, its economic pressures and its focus on the nuclear family as the primary source of affection and care, does not provide an atmosphere in which the serious commitment of friendship can easily be honored. While people do cultivate friendly relationships, we do not often publicly reflect, as did Aelred, on the nature and blessings of friendship itself. We certainly do not often hear it mentioned in most pastoral contexts—in preaching, teaching or counseling settings. And we are not often given an opportunity to think about our friends as the earthen vessels in which we carry God's love.

The historical moments in which Aelred, Francis and Jane lived were periods characterized by their humanistic ethos. The human experience was taken seriously in the life of the spirit as well as in theology, philosophy and the arts. This was significant precisely because the Christian tradition's tendency in matters spiritual usually was (and often still is) to see spiritual concerns as separate from what is most human. The spiritual life is thus conceived as the facet or mode of life that avoids or triumphs over the "merely" human.

It is the genius of Francis, Aelred, Jane and others of like mind to perceive that we come to God not in bypassing those persons and created things that we love, but precisely *through* them. They believed that it is not that we love God and then, as a result, turn to others as secondary loves, nor that our deep love of others is intrinsically a distraction or a hindrance to our love of God. No. The two loves—human and divine—are intimately intertwined. Jane gave lyrical expression to this thought in a letter she wrote in 1634, a decade after Francis' death, to Noel Brulart, Commandeur du Sillery, a wealthy patron of the order of the Visitation which she and Francis had founded.

> My very honored and most dearly beloved brother,
>
> ...You wouldn't believe how much comfort it gives me to know that you are praying for me. To my knowledge, I don't think I ever fail to remember you, especially at holy communion, and I never want to fail in this. I am sure that the merit of holy communion is a worthy response to the genuine, incomparable love God has given you for our blessed Father [the late Francis de Sales] and his dear Visitation, and for myself in particular, it seems, even though I don't deserve it. Really, as imperfect as I am, God has willed to unite my heart intimately with yours; for this I shall ever bless His

divine goodness.

...God be praised for all His graces, especially for having given you a heart which, in my opinion, is fashioned after His own most sacred one. In truth, my very dear brother, your heart is capable of touching ours by its incomparable love. Apparently, you have drawn this love from the inexhaustible love of our divine Savior, for neither human considerations nor the power of nature could bring about anything like it. It is the most precious gift imaginable.[3]

We learn to love both God and others at the same time. It is as if our hearts undergo expansion in the very process of loving itself; they become capable of more generous and creative love in whatever direction it is focused. Being in relationships challenges and changes us, turns us inside out and lays us bare. As we grow in love of others, our capacity for loving God increases. As we fall more deeply in love with God, we grow more open to others. Our retreat directors knew this. And they knew that friendship was one of the privileged forms of love.

For Reflection

- *Bring to mind the friendships you have shared during your life. Pick one or two and recall their progress, savoring their details.*

- *What has been the most important quality of your close friendships? How have they brought you closer to God?*

- *Our guides define friendship as a love characterized by mutuality and equality. How have you experienced this truth?*

- *Imagine yourself as Francis or Jane or Aelred. A very pious person in town who is respected as an authority in spiritual matters has just preached a sermon or related a vision that says that loving family or friends or others can keep us from loving God. How do you respond? Perhaps you could dramatize this in a group, choosing characters to portray.*

For Further Reflection and Discussion

If any begin to give themselves to God, there are so many to criticize them that they need to seek companionship to defend themselves until they are so strong that it is no longer a burden for them to suffer this criticism. And if they don't seek this companionship they will find themselves in much difficulty.... For in falling I had many friends to help me; but in rising I found myself so alone that I am now amazed I did not remain forever fallen.[4]— Teresa of Avila

Closing Prayer

Loving God,
you create us
and sustain us in love.
You bring many people
into our lives.
Some of them we love—
parents, sisters,
children, brothers,
grandparents, lovers,
partners, friends.
May we acknowledge

these loves as gifts from you,
our loving creator.
May we cherish each love
and help it to grow.
Especially, may we cherish
the gift of our friends.
For they hollow out our hearts
in a way that no other love does,
making our hearts hollows
where we uncover
our shared love of you.

Notes

1 Aelred of Rievaulx, *Spiritual Friendship*. Cistercian Fathers Series, Number Five. Trans. Mary Eugenia Laker, S.S.N.D. (Washington, D.C.: Cistercian Publications, 1974), pp. 53-55.

2 Ibid., pp. 72-73.

3 Wendy M. Wright, "That Is What It is Made For: The Image of the Heart in the Spirituality of Francis de Sales and Jane de Chantal" in *Spiritualities of the Heart*, ed. Annice Callahan, R.S.C.J. (Mahwah, N.J.: Paulist Press, 1990), p. 151.

4 Life 7.22, *The Collected Works of St. Teresa of Avila*, Vol. I, trans. Kieran Kavanaugh and Otilio Rodriguez (Washington, D.C.: The Washington Province of Discalced Carmelites, ICS Publications, 1976).

DAY THREE

The Friendship Which Is Spiritual

Coming Together in the Spirit

> I give you a new commandment:
> love one another;
> you must love one another
> just as I have loved you.
> It is by your love for one another,
> that everyone will recognise you
> as my disciples. (John 13:34-35, NJB)

Hold this fragment of God's love letter in your heart. Let it be the baseline that supports the melody of today's retreat.

Defining Our Thematic Content

All the loves of which the human heart is capable have Divine Love as their root and source. The very capacity to love is intrinsic to human beings because they are created in the image and likeness of God who is Love itself. One special love, the love of spiritual friends, is unique. It is a love, as Aelred says, "begun in Christ, continued in Christ, and perfected in Christ." With such a view of friendship it would be impossible to dismiss a serious relationship as one in which the pair were "just friends."

It was just such a serious relationship that enabled a woman deemed "the most influential Catholic of the twentieth century" to find her true vocation. Many Americans recognize the name of Dorothy Day, peacemaker, advocate of the poor and cofounder of the Catholic Worker Movement. Not so many knew of Peter Maurin. Peter seemed to drop out of the sky, an answer to Dorothy's anguished prayer at a critical moment in her life. She was struggling with her deeply felt sense of solidarity with the workers, the poor. In her former life, before the birth of her daughter and her conversion to Catholicism, she had aligned herself with the plight of the poor, as a journalist and a supporter of Socialist causes.

Now, cut off from her former associates as a convert, she ached to integrate her religious devotion and her love of the underprivileged. Yet she saw no way to do that in the socially apathetic Church of her day. In her impatience, she gave the problem up to God, begging that she might find a way to respond to the desires she felt were rooted in God's own love. When she returned home to her apartment at the end of the day, Peter Maurin was waiting for her. A vagabond French philosopher-visionary, Peter was full of a vision of a new sort of revolution that could transform the world, a personalist revolution based on the principles of Christ, a revolution of the individual human heart that would enable each person to see each other person as Christ.

Radical hospitality, voluntary poverty, a cultivation of community based on the land—these were the basics of the vision. Dorothy invited him in. She became the journalist, the activist, the one who transformed Peter's program into action. Peter was her mentor, her visionary friend. The love they shared was rooted in God, in the radical, risky love of others and a mutual surrender to the imperative of the gospel. Their friendship was forged from their "harsh and dreadful" fall into the hands of the living God of Love.

Opening Prayer

> God of Love,
> teach us that the many ways
>   we love one another
> are ways that we also love you.
>
> God of Friendship,
> teach us to acknowledge our friendships
>   as loves
> that we must cherish.
>
> God of Love,
> teach us to know you not only
>   as father, mother and brother
> but as our dearest friend.

RETREAT SESSION THREE

Even though friendship is a form of love and even though love is of God, our directors knew, as we all do, that whatever its ultimate source, any human relationship can be either deep or shallow, intentional or haphazard. And so it is with friendship. There is a commonsense way in which we all understand that casual phrase, "Oh, we are just friends." Many of our so-called friends are in fact acquaintances, or they are "friends" because they work at the same company or live on the same block or have children at our children's school. We see them at PTA meetings and soccer matches, and we call them about the curfew for the senior prom. Or they are "friends" because they sing in the same choir or belong to the same bridge club or enjoy the same hobbies that we do.

Beyond these acquaintance-friends, we have friends who are closer to us. Perhaps they are long-term companions who have shared our joys and sorrows through the exigencies of marriages and child-rearing. Perhaps they are intimates with whom we share a deep delight in music or dance. Perhaps they are colleagues with whom we have collaborated on some business or creative venture. Perhaps they are our basketball buddies or the neighbors with whom we meet over coffee in the kitchen or the deeper soul mates with whom we meet in a support group.

Our directors knew that there are types of friendship distinguished by the content of the exchange as well as by their intimacy. They knew that there were some friendships based on the mutual love of God and a shared commitment to deepen in the life of faith. These they called spiritual friendships.

Francis de Sales devoted a great deal of attention to the topic of spiritual friendship in his *Introduction to the Devout Life*. The book was written for laypeople as an aid to developing a life attentive and responsive to the presence of God. He was convinced that such a life was greatly encouraged by friends who shared the same goal. Spiritual friendships are essential, especially for men and women whose daily occupations do not allow them to engage in activities that are overtly religious or to consort with others who take seriously the ways of God. Such friendships act as beacons on the fog-shrouded shoreline toward which we row. Francis saw these as "true friendship" and gave them pride of place in the life of devotion.

> Love everyone, Philothea, with a great, charitable love, but have no friendship except for those that communicate with you in the things of virtue. The more exquisite the virtues that are the matter of your communications, the more perfect shall your friendship also be. If this communication be in the sciences, the friendship is certainly very commendable; but still more so if it be in virtues, in prudence, discretion, fortitude, and justice. Should your mutual and reciprocal communications relate to charity, devotion, and Christian perfection, O God, how precious will this friendship be! It will be excellent, because it comes from God; excellent, because it tends to God; excellent, because its very bond is God; excellent, because it shall last eternally in God. Oh, how good it is to love on earth as they love in heaven; and to learn to cherish one another in this world as we shall do eternally in the next!
> I speak not here of that simple love of charity which we must have for all men, but of that spiritual friendship, by which two, three or more souls communicate one to another their devotion and spiritual affections, and make themselves have but one spirit. Such happy souls may justly sing: "Behold how good and pleasant it is for brethren to dwell together in unity!" Yes, for the delicious balm of devotion distills out of one heart into another by so continual a participation that it may be said that God has poured out upon this friendship "His blessing and life for evermore." I consider all other friendships as but so many shadows in comparison with this, and that their bonds are but chains of glass or jet in comparison with this bond of holy

devotion, which is all of gold. Make no other kind of
friendship than this. I mean the friendships you
make for yourselves; for you must not forsake or
neglect the friendships that nature or previous
duties oblige you to cultivate with your parents,
kindred, benefactors, neighbors, and others. I am
speaking of those which you yourself choose.[1]

Francis de Sales knew that relationships do not simply
support us, they shape us as well. We are constantly
growing and changing in all dimensions of life. Our
spiritual lives are no exception. Too often we assume that
the religious lessons of our school days have equipped us
to meet the challenges of later life. Nothing could be
farther from the truth. Faith is not static. It is dynamic.
And our sense of God and things spiritual ripens as life
presents us with deeper, more complex experiences. The
friends we choose and the content of exchange in our
friendships profoundly influence us. Thus to the extent
that we nurture friendships steeped in the love of God,
we nurture God's growth in us.

Perhaps it might be thought-provoking to think about
spiritual friendship as an art form. Such a relationship is,
on the one hand, a gratuitous gift; on the other, an
intentional creation. To an extent, we are the architects or
sculptors of our own lives. Not that we can control the
events about us. But we generally can have a say in how
we respond to such events. And we can be agents of
choice in our relationships. We can bring our creative
vision to the complex give and take of friendship and
sculpt a dynamic and God-directed union. Certainly
there need be nothing stereotypic or overly pious about
such an understanding.

Nor should such friendships be stilted or other-
worldly. Any vigorous friendship engages the whole

person and is concerned with all aspects of the partners' lives. They need not avoid the gritty and earthy realities of all our lives. But they can turn over the grit and earth to discover the texture of God's grace as it is manifested there. This is an artful undertaking.

Spiritual friendships can and should be as different as the persons engaged in them. But they are always life-changing and life-affirming. And they bind the friends in a union whose deepest bond is greater than themselves. They participate in Love itself. Bishop Francis de Sales knew this well when he wrote to Jane de Chantal shortly after their initial encounter at the Lenten sermons in Dijon. She was drawn to open her heart to him, to confide in him her growing passion to belong only to God. But she felt confusion about the chaotic impulses she had experienced since her husband's death.

Francis knew that in their reaching out in friendship, he and Jane mirrored for one another their widest capacities as human beings and encouraged one another in the necessary expansion to realize those capacities. He explained this to her in a letter written in June 1604.

> I have never intended for there to be any connection between us that carries any obligation except that of love and true Christian friendship, whose binding force Saint Paul calls "the bond of perfection." And truly it is just that, for it is indissoluble and will not slacken. All other bonds are temporary, even that of vows of obedience which are broken by death and other occurrences. But the bond of love grows in time and takes on new power by enduring. It is exempt from the severance of death whose scythe cuts down everything except love: "Love is as strong as death and more powerful than hell," Solomon says.... This is our bond, these are our chains which, the more they restrain and press upon

us, the more they give us ease and liberty. Their
power is only sweetness, their force only gentleness,
nothing is so pliable, nothing so solid as they are.
Therefore, consider me intimately linked with you
and do not be anxious to understand more about it
except that this bond is not contrary to any other
bond, whether it be of a vow or of marriage.[2]

This "bond of perfection" that Francis and Jane shared
was the vessel which carried them together home to God.
The relationship that these two seventeenth-century
figures shared was particular. It began in spiritual
direction and expanded to the point where the two
cofounded a religious congregation. This certainly is not
the only model of spiritual friendship. In fact, it is
certainly conditioned by the ethos of the time in which
our friends lived.

Today we are likely to seek religious guidance from
trained professionals: pastors, counselors, ministers or
spiritual directors. The benefits we gain from such
helping relationships are great. But generally, they do not
qualify as true spiritual friendships (although there are
some exceptions to this). For as caring as they may be,
they do not involve an entity that is mutual and equal.
Instead the model tends to be therapeutic with self-
disclosure taking place on one side only.

The mutual and equal love of friends might occur
more readily today between persons who collaborate in
ministry or who first meet in a faith-sharing group. It
might have its origins in a time of crisis when one or both
of the friends faces grief, illness or loss. It might be a
single-sex friendship or a dual-sex friendship such as the
one shared by Francis and Jane. It might occur between
family members or between persons from very different
cultural and geographical areas.

Whatever the origin and particulars of the bond, all of these friendships are characterized by their mutuality and equality and by the primary content of their exchange: They are about spiritual growth and the increasing love of God and others. Jane herself described the quality of these relationships when she wrote to her spiritual daughters in the community of the Visitation.

> Ah, my dear sisters, our beloved Visitation is a tiny kingdom of charity. If union and holy cherishing do not reign, it will soon be divided and consequently, laid waste, losing the luster which all the ingenuity of human effort could never regain.... Let us therefore all pray that the Spirit of Love, uniter of hearts, grant us this close and living union with God by the total dependence of our will to His and between us by a perfect cherishing and reciprocal union of heart and spirit....[3]

For Reflection

- *What friendships have you shared that could be considered "spiritual friendships"?*

- *Have you chosen or are you drawn to friends because their love of God mirrors your own? How have you nurtured or conducted those friendships?*

- *Friendships are also gifts as well as being intentional. How have you gratefully received and acknowledged the spiritual friends in your life?*

- *Write a letter to a spiritual friend expressing how you feel about the relationship and what it has meant to you.*

- *In a group, imagine you are Aelred of Rievaulx and his*

monastic brothers taking a walk and engaging in dialogue about friendship. What sort of questions or concerns would the brothers raise? How would Aelred respond? Dramatize this scene.

For Further Reflection and Discussion

When Christ said to his disciples: "Love one another" it was not attachment he was laying down as their rule. As it was a fact that there were bonds between them due to the thoughts, the life and the habits they shared, he commanded them to transform these bonds into friendship....

Since, shortly before his death, Christ gave this as a new commandment to be added to the two great commandments of the love of our neighbor and the love of God, we can think that pure friendship, like the love of our neighbor, has in it something of a sacrament. Christ perhaps wished to suggest this with reference to Christian friendship when he said: "Where there are two or three gathered together in my name there am I in the midst of them." Pure friendship is an image of the original and perfect friendship that belongs to the Trinity and is the very essence of God. It is impossible for two human beings to be one while scrupulously respecting the distance that separates them, unless God is present in each of them. The point at which parallels meet is infinity.[4]—Simone Weil

Closing Prayer

Gracious God,
you gift us with friends,
people who shape and change us.
May we choose friends well.
May we tenderly cherish
and tend those friendships
which bring us closer to you.

Teach us not to be afraid
of changing and growing.
Give us the boldness
to risk being opened up
and opened out
so that we might
become what we were
intended to be.

Notes

[1] Francis de Sales, *Introduction to the Devout Life*, trans. John K. Ryan (Garden City, N.Y.: Doubleday Image Books, 1955), pp. 169-170.

[2] Wendy M. Wright, *Bond of Perfection: Jeanne de Chantal and François de Sales* (New York: Paulist Press, 1985), p. 140.

[3] Ibid., p. 140.

[4] Simone Weil, *Waiting for God*, trans. Emma Craufurd (New York: G.P. Putnam's Sons, 1951), p. 208.

Day Four
Friends False and True

Coming Together in the Spirit

> Faithful friends are a sturdy shelter;
>   whoever finds one has found a treasure.
> Faithful friends are beyond price;
>   no amount can balance their worth.
> Faithful friends are life-saving medicine;
>   and those who fear the Lord will find them.
> Those who fear the Lord direct their friendship
>   aright,
>   for as they are, so are their neighbors also.
> (Sirach 6:14-17, NRSV)

Sing the refrain of this love song until it becomes the music of your heart.

Defining Our Thematic Content

Just as there are many types of love, so there are many types of friendship. The friendship that is rooted in love of God and has as its aim the deepening of that love is a spiritual friendship. Such relationships are life-changing and life-affirming. They shape us. They plunge us into the hidden recesses of our hearts where our deepest joy is found, inviting us into new experiences of divine and human intimacy. Their bonds, forged as they are in freedom, give us the liberty to discover God anew.

How crucial these bonds of spiritual friendship are is well-illustrated by the ancient Celtic Christian who said, "Anyone without a soul-friend is a body without a head." The soul-friend or *anmchara* was a charismatic counselor and guide. In pre-Christian days, every Celtic chief had his druid advisor in matters of the spirit, and the tradition seems to have survived and been transformed with the coming of Christianity. We know that Saints Columba and Brigit and Comgall, all luminaries in the Celtic Church, had *anmchara* or served as such for others. Soul friends came from any walk of life, they could be clerics or laypersons, women or men. The soul friend was the one to whom you poured out the secrets of your heart and who had the gift of discretion, the ability to discern the various movements of the spirit that motivate, prompt and inform the friends of God.

Perhaps it is not surprising that the practice of sacramental confession as we know it today has its roots in the Celtic Church where Christians had learned that to spill out one's heart to a friend was the surest way to reconciliation with God. The Celtic soul friend was not a formal, sacramental relationship, as that between priest and penitent in today's Church. But the relationship was sacramental in the widest sense of the term. It rendered the invisible visible. It provided a channel for God's grace to flow into the heart. It was rooted in and gave access to the love of God.

Opening Prayer

Giving God,
you fill our lives
 with many gifts.
Among those gifts
 are the persons we call friends.

Weighing God,
grant us the gift of discerning
 the reasons why
we call each other friend.

Sifting God,
give us fingers and hearts
 that can open wide
to let the false friends
 filter through.

RETREAT SESSION FOUR

As we have seen, Aelred of Rievaulx and Francis de Sales in their respective centuries and their respective contexts (Aelred writing for his monastic brethren and Francis writing for a wider group of devout laypersons, especially women) praised the virtues and beauty of friendship. Both also recognized the specific form of friendship—spiritual friendship—that has as its motive and content the increasing love of God.

At the same time that their enthusiasm for friendly relations was great, Aelred and Francis were both very discriminating about the variety of motives and goals that could bind two persons together with the name "friend." In fact, these cautions were not simply asides, but occupied both writers to a significant extent.

Alongside his discussion of spiritual friendship, Bishop de Sales placed an extended discussion of "evil and frivolous" friendships and "fond loves." Because friendship is a form of love that necessarily involves communication, the nature of that communication must be assessed when evaluating the friendship.

> According to the diversity of communications, friendship also differs, and the communications differ according to the variety of the goods that they communicate to each other. If they be false and vain goods, the friendship is also false and vain. If they be true goods, the friendship is likewise true. The more excellent the goods may be, the more excellent also is the friendship. For as that honey is best which is gathered from the blossoms of the most exquisite flowers, so that love which is founded upon the most exquisite communication is the most excellent. There is honey at Heraclea in Pontus that is poisonous and deprives those that eat it of reason, because it is gathered from the aconite, which abounds in that country. Even so the friendship that is grounded upon the communication of false and vicious goods is altogether false and vicious.[1]

Francis criticized friendship forged on the basis of what he termed "the exchange of sensual pleasures," in other words, external beauty, pleasing characteristics or accomplishments. The bishop was well aware that it is easy to be attracted to people because of their physical appeal, fine clothes, sports ability, outgoing personality, or keen sense of humor and to attach oneself because one wishes one had these things oneself. Apparently in the courtly circles of his day, such liaisons were common. He saw them as the particular temptation of the young.

He warned too of "fond loves," affectionate attachments especially among persons of the opposite sex, which delight in the game of flirtatious attentions. Charmed by the pleasure of toying with each other, of engaging in "wishes, desires, sighs, amorous entertainments" and such, these relationships are, in Francis' mind, "phantoms of friendships" deserving of neither the name of friendship nor of love. The Genevan bishop conjures up for us a vision of courtly pastimes that lend themselves to abuse. Their allurements he vigorously dismisses.

> The walnut tree is very harmful to the vines and fields in which it is planted. It is so large that it attracts all the moisture of the surrounding earth and renders it incapable of nourishing the other plants. Its leaves are also so thick that they make a large and close shade. Lastly, it allures passers-by to it, who, to knock down its fruit, spoil and trample upon everything about it. These fond loves do the same injury to the soul. They possess her in such manner and so strongly draw her motions to themselves, that she has no strength left to produce any good work. Their leaves, namely, their idle talk, their amusements, and their dalliance, are so frequent, that all leisure time is squandered away on them. Finally, they engender so many temptations, distractions, suspicions, and other effects that the whole heart is trampled down and destroyed by them. In a word, these fond loves not only banish heavenly love but also the fear of God from the soul. They weaken the mind and they ruin reputation. In a word they are the sport of courts, but the plague of hearts.[2]

The abbot of Rievaulx has similar criticisms to make of relationships forged from questionable motives—he calls them "childlike," aimless relationships—but his cautions also reflect his own experience of ambitious men forging alignments based on the mutual advantage of wealth, status or fame. Advantage may, and often does, accrue from friendship, Aelred knows, but it should proceed from it, not be the motive for its cultivation. Aelred goes further than Francis in delineating the discrimination needed to assess whether a friendship should be pursued or not. The abbot's considerations, no doubt odd sounding to many modern ears, indicate the seriousness with which he accepted the bonds of friendship. Book Three of *On Spiritual Friendship* is thus entitled "The Condition and Characters Requisite for Unbroken Friendship" and delineates the four stages through which the discernment of a true friend should ideally proceed. The stages are selection, probation, admission and perfect harmony.

The selection process involves assessing the character of a potential friend. Aelred and his dialogue partners Walter and Gratian turn the issues over thoughtfully.

> **Aelred:** First of all, then, let us deal with selection itself. Now there are certain vices such that, if anyone has been involved in them, he will not long preserve the laws or rights of friendship. Persons of this type should not readily be chosen for friendship; but if their life and habits be found pleasing in other respects, one should deal energetically with them, to the end that they may be healed and so considered fitted for friendship. Such persons are, for example, the irascible, the fickle, the suspicious, and the garrulous. Indeed, it is difficult for one subject to the frenzy of anger not to rise up sometime against his friend, as it is written in

Ecclesiasticus: "There is a friend that will disclose hatred and strife and reproaches." Therefore Scripture says: "Be not a friend to an angry man, and do not walk with a furious man, lest he become a snare for your soul." And Solomon: "Anger rests in the bosom of a fool." And who does not think it impossible to preserve friendship for long with a fool?

Walter: But we have seen you, if we are not mistaken, with deep devotion cultivate a friendship with a very irascible man, and we have heard, he was never hurt by you even to the end of his life, though he often offended you.

Aelred: There are some individuals who have a natural bent toward anger, yet who are accustomed so to restrain and overcome this passion that they never give way to those five vices which Scripture testifies dissolve and break friendship. However they may occasionally offend a friend by a thoughtless word or act or by a zeal that fails in discretion. If it happens that we have received such men into our friendship, we must bear with them patiently. And since their affection toward us is established with certainty, if then there is any excess in word or action, this ought to be put up with as being in a friend, or at least our admonition of his fault ought to be administered painlessly and even pleasantly.

Gratian: A few days ago that friend of yours, whom many think you prefer to all of us, was, so we thought, overcome by anger, and said and did something that everyone could see displeased you. Yet we do not believe or see that he has in any degree lost favor with you. Hence we are not a little surprised that, when we speak together, you will not neglect anything that pleases him no matter how trivial it may be, yet he cannot bear even trifles for your sake.

Walter: Gratian is far bolder than I am; for I was aware of these facts, but knowing your feeling toward him, I did not dare say anything to you about the matter.

Aelred: Certainly that man is very dear to me. Having once received him into my friendship, I can never do otherwise than love him. Therefore, if perhaps I was stronger than he was in this instance, and since the wills of both did not fuse into one, it was easier for me to yield my will than his. And since there was no question of any dishonor being involved, and as confidence was not violated, or virtue lessened, it was right for me to yield to my friend that I might bear with him when he seemed to have transgressed, and that, when his peace was endangered, I might prefer his will to mine.[3]

Aelred and his companions go on to discuss the vices that so injure a friendship as to cause its dissolution. Slander, persecution, excessive pride which refuses to admit guilt, the injuring of loved ones, the breaching of confidences, treachery: These constitute the grounds of terminating a friendship.

Similarly, four positive qualities must be tested in a friend— loyalty, right intention, discretion and patience— so that one might entrust oneself in confidence. Once discernments have been made, a person is found trustworthy to bear the name friend and is admitted to that status, a high expectation of the relationship is held out.

Aelred: This is that extraordinary and great happiness which we await, with God himself acting and diffusing, between himself and his creatures whom he has uplifted, among the very degrees and orders which he has distinguished, among the individual souls whom he has chosen, so much friendship and charity, that thus each loves another as he does himself; and that, by this means, just as each one rejoices in his own, so does he rejoice in the good fortune of another, and thus the happiness of each one individually is the happiness of all, and the universality of all happiness is the possession of each individual. There one finds no hiding of thoughts, no dissembling of affection. This is true and eternal friendship, which begins in this life and is perfected in the next, which here belongs to the few where few are good, but there belongs to all where all are good. Here, probation is necessary since there is a mingling of wise and unwise; there they need no probation, since an angelic and, in a certain manner, divine perfection beautifies them. To this pattern, then, let us compare our friends, whom we are to love as we do ourselves, whose confidences are to be laid bare to us, to whom our confidences are likewise to be disclosed, who are to be firm and stable and constant in all things.[4]

We in the twentieth century might not evaluate our friendships with the same formal criteria that Aelred and his companions delineate for us. But the effort at evaluation itself is worth taking seriously. Not just any sort of friend will do, especially when the life of the spirit is at stake. Not everyone, even if he or she is a regular churchgoer, or even a religious "professional" (for example, clergy or religious educator) is necessarily a potential spiritual friend. It may even be that a pastoral helping relationship is the last context in which we might find a spiritual friend. The complex dynamics of unequal power, or lack of pastoral responsibility, or personal vulnerability can conspire in such relationships to injure rather than heal. We must use our common sense and powers of discrimination to sift and weigh the partnerships into which we entrust ourselves.

For Reflection

- *How do you respond to Francis' and Aelred's assessment of "false" and "true" friendships?*

- *How have you evaluated friendships? What criteria have you found helpful in assessing which friendships bring life and which do not?*

- *What are the characteristics you would expect from a deep spiritual friendship?*

- *Drawing upon your own experience, but fictionalizing it, enact a scenario in which a well-intentioned spiritual friendship takes a turn in another direction. How would Francis or Jane or Aelred counsel you? How might their advice be revised or newly interpreted in the twentieth century?*

For Further Reflection and Discussion

In one session John said, "I have a friend whom I love deeply. To my surprise I also experience resentment toward him now and then. I go out of my way to show my love to him, but he seems to take me often for granted and I have a nagging feeling that I am giving too much. I do not like myself for that."

"There is too much goodwill in you," Tony remarked, "too much spirituality, and you get tied down. In friendship one must be able to say the following: I accept you, I'll support you, you can count on me. And I want you to reciprocate my love. I want you to be honest with me."[5]—Anthony de Mello

Closing Prayer

God,
you have called us friend
and you have asked us to love one another
just the way we have been loved by you.

We ask you
to teach us what that is.
We ask you to guide us as we
grope our way into the fullness
of love.

Uncover the motives
we hide from,
unmask the pretenses that shield us,
disarm our defenses,
so that when we love one another
it will be at least a little bit the way
that we have been loved by you.

Notes

1 *Introduction to the Devout Life*, p. 165.

2 Ibid., p. 169.

3 *On Spiritual Friendship*, pp. 94-95.

[4] *On Spiritual Friendship*, p. 111.

[5] Anthony de Mello, S.J., *We Heard the Bird Sing* (Chicago: Loyola University Press, 1995), p. 34.

DAY FIVE
Passionate Friends

Coming Together in the Spirit

> When David had finished speaking to Saul, the soul
> of Jonathan was bound to the soul of David, and
> Jonathan loved him as his own soul. Saul took him
> that day and would not let him [David] return to his
> father's house. Then Jonathan made a covenant with
> David, because he loved him as his own soul.
> Jonathan stripped himself of the robe that he was
> wearing, and gave it to David, and his armor, and
> even his sword and his bow and his belt. (1 Samuel
> 18:1-4, NRSV)

Imagine stripping yourself of all that you have to give it
to another. Let this image suffuse your retreat this day.

Defining Our Thematic Content

Discriminating between true and false friendships is
part of the discerning spirit that is needed to nurture and
sustain a God-centered relationship. Not every person or
situation lends itself to the mutuality and equality that
friendship implies. Not every friendship has at its explicit
core the love of God. Rare and precious, such friendships
help us hollow out the God-shaped space which God

alone can fill. They change us into the image and likeness of the One in whose image we are created. They take us home together to the source of love.

Our Christian tradition records many beautiful and passionate friendships in which love of God burned and bound two human hearts. Stories like the following may expand our appreciation of the theme we are together exploring.

Her name was Diana. His was Jordan. She was from Andalo. He from Saxony. Jordan was the successor to the generalship of the Dominican order after the death of Dominic and came to know of Diana from his predecessor. It seems that Diana, a young Lombard woman of notable lineage with a passion for the contemplative life, had for several years attempted to enter religious life, much to the dismay of her family. Under Dominic's guidance she had led a mortified life in her home and gathered about her a group of women followers. Refused admission to a nearby convent, she planned a country outing with friends, in the course of which she sought refuge with a community of Augustinian canonesses. Enraged, her brothers dragged her physically from the property and confined her to her room for one year. But Diana's determination was undaunted.

At this time Jordan entered the scene. Through his efforts she became a member of the Dominican family and succeeded in establishing herself and a small band of friends in the convent of Saint Agnes, thereby founding the Second Order of Saint Dominic. Jordan and Diana exchanged a series of letters throughout the years 1222-1237 which attest to the depth of their relationship. One quotation from Jordan must suffice to give some flavor of this friendship:

You are so deeply engraven on my heart that the
more I realize how truly you love me from the
depths of your soul, the more incapable I am of
forgetting you and the more constantly you are in
my thoughts; for your love of me moves me
profoundly and makes my love for you burn more
strongly....[1]

By maintaining their relationship as spiritual friends,
neither becoming lovers or spouses nor retreating into
the safety of distant acquaintances, Diana of Andalo and
Jordan of Saxony embodied some of the gifts and
dynamics of both marriage and celibacy.

Opening Prayer

Passionate God,
we have hearts that
long for each other.
We have hearts that
long for you.

Thank you for the inner aching
and longing
that keep us seeking
your love.

Thank you for the passion
which propels us out of ourselves
and into each other's hearts.

May our passion for one another
fuel our deeper
passion for you
and hollow out in us that God-shaped space
which only you can fill.

Retreat Session Five

Our Christian tradition is full of wonderful stories: biblical accounts, saints' lives, tales of remarkable events and happenings. Some of the most arresting stories are about friends, women and men who together have charted new ways of being human in response to the gospel invitation. Jane de Chantal and Francis de Sales are two such friends. The details of their relationship are engaging, and we will recount some of its highlights. But even more engaging are the general dynamics of that friendship and the insight into the dynamics of going to God that it gives to modern seekers. This will be the subject of our retreat for the next few days.

In an article I wrote several years ago, I reflected on the power and deep wisdom to be discerned in well-balanced spiritual friendships between men and women. However, I cautioned readers:

> But there are also times when a person is drawn lovingly toward someone of the opposite sex with whom it is neither appropriate nor prudent to express the full range of the compelling intimacy he or she feels. Such an attraction goes well beyond infatuation or admiration and is arresting precisely because it is the spiritual dimension of the bond that is the most central. That special man, that remarkable woman, is attractive because of his or her prayerfulness, spiritual wisdom, sense of shared Christian vision. He or she knows the hopes of my heart in God, senses what in me is leaning toward

my best and fullest self, what is most precious or
urgent to me.*

In such friendships, both partners must have a well-
rooted sense of self and a strong commitment to their
primary vocation. Each needs to respect the context in
which the other lives (their home or community life,
other commitments and concerns). The two must also be
rooted in a community of faith in which their common
vision of God and discipleship is nourished.

Now we turn to the highlights of the friendship
between Jane de Chantal and Francis de Sales.

The two friends first met in 1604 when they were in
their early thirties. Francis was the bishop of Geneva, a
rising star of the ecclesial and spiritual renewal taking
place in France in the early part of the century. Jane was
the baroness de Chantal, a young widow whose shattered
former identity was slowly being reassembled in an
unanticipated way. She was seeking a spiritual director
who could help her make sense of her chaotic feelings
about her vocation. He was a pastoral leader who offered
spiritual direction. But he was also a man whose heart
was hungry for God and open to hearts equally hungry.
Their meeting at the Lenten series was thus ripe with
possibility.

Although Jane had for a time been under the spiritual
guidance of a local priest, the deepest questions she
harbored were not being addressed. The warmth and
passion of the vision Francis presented in his sermons
drew her as did the graciousness of his person. He, on his
side, noted her attentiveness. When they were introduced

* Reprinted from *Weavings: A Journal of the Christian Spiritual Life*
(July/August, 1987), Vol. III., No. 4. Copyright ©1987 by The Upper
Room. Used by permission.

and he learned a bit of her history, he, too, was drawn. Soon they entered into a formal spiritual guidance relationship. It was the custom of the time to take such relationships with utmost seriousness, ban they both prayed earnestly before they bound themselves in covenant in the sight of God.

During the first years of their relationship there was asymmetry. Jane was the directee, Francis the director. Yet even in this early period when the focus was upon discerning God's will for the young widow, the depth and intimacy of their pairing was evident. Francis wrote to Jane within months of their first meeting about the affection he had for her.

> ...from the first time that you consulted me about your interior life, God granted me a great love for your spirit. When you confessed to me in greater detail, a remarkable bond was forged in my soul that caused me to cherish your soul more and more. This made me write to you that God had given me to you, not thinking that it would ever be possible for the affection that I felt in my spirit to be increased— especially by praying to God for you. But now, my dear Daughter, a certain new quality has emerged which it seems I cannot describe, only its effect is a greater interior sweetness that I have to wish for you a perfect love of God and other spiritual blessings. No, I am not exaggerating the truth in the least, I speak before "my heart's God" and yours. Each affection is different from others. The one I have for you has a certain quality which consoles me infinitely and, if all were known, is extremely profitable to me. Consider this an absolute truth and have no more doubts about it.[2]

That Jane felt deeply about the relationship we have no

doubt, but through the accidents of history, we have lost much of her part of their correspondence. Nevertheless, we can chart the course of their friendship. For years, while her children were growing, Jane continued living with her father-in-law or father and practicing the sort of domestic devotion that Francis had advocated in his *Introduction to the Devout Life*. All the while, Jane listened intently to what she felt was God's prompting to "leave the world" and enter religious life.

Jane's and Francis' friendship during these years was, as suggested, somewhat asymmetrical. His position as her director and her senior in spiritual matters necessitated this. However, more and more the bishop and the widow found themselves to be mutually engaged. Francis' letters reflect the two friends' growing identity based on their shared love of God and commitment to the life of the spirit. That their friendship had its roots in the spiritual realm is reflected in the merging of their story with the greater story of Christian faith. Francis wrote:

> After all, I never say the Holy Mass without you and whatever concerns you most deeply. I do not receive the sacrament at all without you. In the end, I am as much yours as you could ever wish.[3]

Similarly,

> ...it is true, my dear daughter, our unity is utterly consecrated to the highest unity and each day I sense more vividly the truth of our sincere connection which will not let me ever forget you even long, long after I have forgotten myself in order to better attach myself to the Cross.[4]

The language of their letters more and more became the

language of love. But a caution should be added here. In their era, such language tended to be much more effusive than our common epistolary language. There was a literary tradition of correspondence between friends which allowed for an exuberant yet appropriate expression of sentiment. There was also a mystical tradition that explored the love of God through the nuptial metaphors of the Song of Songs. In this tradition the soul became the bride ardently seeking her divine beloved who in turn sought her in passionate pursuit. Such tradition gave a literary framework for the exploration of their friendship.

> You would not believe how much my heart was strengthened by our resolutions and by everything that contributed to their establishment. I feel an extraordinary sweetness about them as likewise I feel for the love I bear you. Because I love that love incomparably. It is strong, resilient, measureless and unreserved yet gentle, pliant, completely pure and tranquil. In short, if I am not deceived, it is completely in God.[5]

Francis was aware, however, that not everyone would comprehend the bond that was being forged between them. His concern was slight that she would misread his meanings, but he was aware that others might misconstrue.

> I am willing that you could communicate the advice I have given you about your conscience to your confessor. But not the letters which are a little too unguarded and cordial to be seen by other than the simplest eyes and which express my utterly frank and open intentions in your regard.[6]

The friendship Jane and Francis shared was passionate. It was also transformative. This is always a possibility in such unions. Passion, like asceticism, oddly enough can destabilize the intact world a person has created for him or herself. In the process of destabilization new possibilities present themselves. New ways of perceiving and being, new ways of thinking and acting become possible. Most of us construct lives and identities that have very little or no room for God. Even if we are serious about the spiritual quest, we generally operate within a framework which includes only the possibilities we have already envisioned. Disruptions in our carefully guarded worlds create a breach into which God's mercy can enter. Passionate friendships can be one such disruption, catapulting us into vulnerability and from there, into growth and change. Part of that change involved increased self-knowledge for both partners, as well as increased desire to love and serve God in new and adventurous ways.

The bishop's and the widow's friendship continued to ripen and at last produced fruits beyond itself. Francis had long been fascinated by what he had seen in his student days in Italy: communities of devout women who dedicated themselves to prayer and good works, yet who were not formally vowed to a life of perpetual enclosure and the traditional religious promises of poverty, chastity and obedience. This more flexible model of community would be feasible for women like Jane, whose family responsibilities ruled out the possibility of rigid religious life, as well as women barred from such by ill health, handicaps or temperament. Jane, for her part, longed to give herself utterly to her God. After years of careful discernment, during which they both waited and prayed, they founded the Visitation of Holy Mary.

Friendship, as does all authentic love, ultimately bears

fruit. For the widow and the bishop the fruit was not only their own transformation but a new community that responded to a deeply felt need of the times. They experienced their friendship not as something private, although it was deeply personal, but rather as a part of a larger momentum of love working in the world. They saw themselves as caught up in the dynamics of spiritual renewal animating the Church. That renewal they understood as prompted by the spirit of God. Thus their relationship had many layers. The love of God was at its center, a love that was active in transforming them as well as in transforming the world.

Between themselves they experienced that love as profound affectivity. They employed the language of desire to convey to one another the richness of what was occurring between them. Francis expressed it well in one of his letters to his friend.

> You well know, seeing as how I have written to you about it, that I go to you by following the spirit and it is true. No, it will be impossible for anything to ever separate me from your soul. The bond is too strong. Death itself would not have the power to dissolve it because it is of a quality that lasts forever.[7]

For Reflection

- *What is your experience of passionate friendship? How has it led you closer to God?*

- *What does Francis de Sales mean when he claims that "each affection is different from others"? What has been your experience in this regard?*

- *What are the levels and dimensions of a love that is grounded in God? How have you experienced this in your own life?*

- *What have been the fruits of the friendships with which you have been graced?*

- *In a group, share Scripture passages, poems, music or art that speak to you of the passionate love of friends.*

For Further Reflection and Discussion

For the wider community spiritual friendships shared by men and women can be eschatological signs. They reveal a Christian perception of the goodness of all creation and the blessedness of all human love which finds its true source and end in God. As such they show forth a love that is respectful of all the myriad ties of care and service that otherwise bind people....

Similarly, they can be signs of a visionary Christian community because they bespeak a radical mutuality and equality between persons. Such friendships can be signs that, as St. Paul says, 'in Christ there is neither male nor female,' not in the sense that one's God-given sexuality is erased but that the sexes are not necesarily divided against each other but rather gathered up together in their full distinctiveness and brought to God.[8]

Closing Prayer

Loving God,
you lead us in love

to one another.
May the passion that we feel
for you
enflame our love of one another.
May the passion that we know
for one another
always take its flame from you.

You have told us that
we are the branches
and you the vine.
May we bear the fruit
that ripens when we
engraft ourselves in you.

Notes

[1] Gerald Vann, *To Heaven With Diana! A Study of Jordan of Saxony and Diana d'Andalo with a Translation of the Letters of Jordan* (Chicago: Henry Regnery, 1965), p. 34.

[2] *Bond of Perfection*, p. 122.

[3] Ibid., p. 123.

[4] Ibid.

[5] Ibid., p. 124.

[6] Ibid., p. 125.

[7] Ibid., pp. 123-124.

[8] Wright, "Reflections," op. cit., p. 23.

Day Six
The Community of Friends

Coming Together in the Spirit

No one has ever seen God,
but as long as we love each other
God remains in us
and his love comes to its perfection in us.
This is the proof that we remain in him
and he in us,
that he has given us a share in his Spirit.
(1 John 4:12-13, NJB)

Let this living, loving word continue to echo in your mind as you enter today's retreat.

Defining Our Thematic Content

The relationship Jane de Chantal and Francis de Sales shared gives us a glimpse into the passionate nature of one spiritual friendship. The love that they felt for one another was deeply entwined with their passion for God and for God's unfolding activity in the world through the Church. Their love was intensely intimate, drawing them together in a union that was eventually fruitful. Their cocreation, the Order of the Visitation, was the issue of a creative spiritual union. The love shared by Francis and Jane is specific to their experience and not all spiritual friendships chart such a course. But some do. And many draw the partners into a union that is growing and ultimately life-transforming.

In the 1980's in the Central American country of Nicaragua a group of peasants met to pray, to ponder the significance of the gospel for their lives. Part of the "base community" movement encouraged by the spirit of liberation theology that swept the Latin American Church in the seventies and eighties, the peasants of Solentiname took the call of spiritual friendship seriously. They came together in a communion that drew its sustenance from God's word. Their friendship in community was as much a relationship of guidance as the soul-friends of the Celtic Church, as much a union of love as the partnership of Jordan of Saxony and Diana of Andalo. They knew that love translates in solidarity and action on behalf of those in need. Their shared reflections on Luke 9:10-17, the multiplication of the loaves, expresses this truth.

> ...**Pancho:** "I'm just catching on to what this means here! They didn't have enough—right?—to feed the five thousand people. But then he says to them: It doesn't matter, share it. And there was more than enough! He made them understand that no matter how little they had they had to share it. And they shared it, and with his power he made it stretch out. The lesson is that no matter how little we have we always have to give."

> **Alejandro:** "As I see it, the same thing didn't happen to Jesus that almost always happens to the church: that it's nothing but words—that we must do good and all that. But when people are hungry,

nothing is done to solve the problem. Christ not only uses words, talking to them all day about the kingdom of God, but he feeds them through his disciples. He doesn't send them away hungry. Christ's gospel also feeds you. But many bishops and priests think it's only to save your soul and not to change the economic situation of society...."

Esperancita: ..."About the fish and the loaves that were so small and they increased and got bigger: that can also be a community that's born tiny and grows and gets to be big because inside it consciousness is growing and love is growing and it gets to be the size of the whole country. I see that in the number of loaves and fishes that it says."[1]

Opening Prayer

God of Love,
you no longer call us servants,
you call us friends.
You draw us to yourself
in a communion of love.

You call us to one another
in a communion that draws us
into the depths of love.

We find ourselves communing
in ever widening circles,
drawn to each other,
a community of friends
whose fount and end is you.

Retreat Session Six

The religious congregation of the Visitation brought into being by the friendship that Jane de Chantal and Francis de Sales shared was unique in its day. It was a community formed specifically for women rather than a women's branch of an existing male order, and it was a community designed for women generally excluded from religious life—widows, the handicapped or the frail of health. Furthermore, the Visitation was a community whose particular charism—or specific reason for being—was the cultivation of gentle, loving relationships in community.

Jesus and the spirit of Jesus were to be manifested in the world through the practice of what Jane and Francis called the "little virtues"—humility, gentleness, patience, simplicity and the like. These little virtues were to be realized unobtrusively, in the daily rounds of living and working together. Everything in the Visitation was structured to facilitate the realization of the little virtues and, by extension, the living spirit of Jesus. Governance and guidance were characterized by gentle persuasion and the "winning of hearts." Gentle speech and demeanor were encouraged as was patient forbearance for each other's weaknesses.

Everything was to be accomplished by love, not force. Similarly, the ties that bound together the various houses of the extended Visitation network were not to be primarily juridical. The Visitation houses were to be bound by love, their conformity born out of mutual acquiescence and regard.

Fragments of letters written by Jane to the superiors of various Visitandine houses provide us with glimpses of the loving cordiality fostered within the congregation.

To be sure, I am convinced, and experience has taught me, that nothing so wins souls as gentleness and cordiality. I beg you, dearest, follow this method, for it is the spirit of our blessed Father [Francis de Sales]. Curtness in words or actions only hardens hearts and depresses them, whereas gentleness encourages them and makes them receptive....[2]

For the love of God, be kind, sincere, trusting, open and communicative with the Sisters, especially with Sister Assistant. And when you find them at times disagreeing with you, consult them simply and bring them around very gently, for in the end they should yield. But, for goodness' sake, dear, win them over through kindness, patience and instruction, asking them to read often our Bishop's [Francis'] conferences, for love wins all. Refer them always to the conferences and to the rule which teach so perfectly what each of you should do.

Yes, my dear, true charity requires us to forget the faults of others in order not to wish them ill, but not to forget them when this would mean jeopardizing the well-being of a community which depends on the good will and wisdom of those who make up the community.[3]

In the same spirit, Jane tenderly exhorted an entire Visitation community to strive for the mutual, harmonious enactment of love.

So, courage, dear ones. May all of you together, and each one in particular, work at this and never grow slack. May you all live in harmony with one heart and mind in God. Do not wish for anything except what your superiors and your Sisters ask of you. Show a childlike trust and gentleness toward one

another, supporting each one in mutual charity.
Never be astonished at the faults of the community
or of any individual Sister, for to be shocked at our
Sisters' faults, to pick them apart, examine them, to
get all upset about them is the sign of a
narrowmindedness which has no insight into
human frailty, and very little charity or forbearance.
That is why those who are inclined to be so
righteous should close their eyes to what is going on
around them and remind themselves constantly that
charity does not go looking for evil, and when she
does come upon it, she looks the other way and
excuses those who commit it. This should be our
attitude toward our Sisters who are our
companions.[4]

Such a community was unique in its day, and reveals to
us a dimension of spiritual friendship that goes beyond
that revealed by the relationship forged by the
congregation's founders. It shows us a community of
friends. Francis and Jane did not directly speak of
individual friendships within the Visitation community.
In fact, in keeping with prevailing thinking, they believed
that one on one, or "particular," friendships were more
suited to life outside community. Within religious
community, favoritism and factionalism could be bred if
community members paired off and kept to themselves.
Instead, a more all-embracing, less "particular" kind of
loving was encouraged.

There are many cogent critiques of such admonitions
against "particular friendships" in religious life,
especially from the hindsight of history. Suffice it to say
that in most twentieth-century religious communities, the
life-enhancing value of genuine friendships, "particular"
or not, is affirmed. The question of exclusivity or
factionalism is now kept separate from the question of

cultivating healthy intimacies. And, in many contemporary communities the issues of intimacy and mission are clearly addressed. Since most groups of this sort are founded for a specific mission—education, service to the poor, the cultivation of a contemplative life—the mission often is the focal point of relationships within community.

For most Christians, however, the faith community in which they find themselves is a good deal less selective and intentional than a religious order. The parish or local congregation often provides the only community available. And most parishes or congregations are much too diverse to be genuine communities of friendship except in the most general sense. Smaller units—a Bible study, a faith-sharing circle, a covenant group, a Christian couples or singles program, a faith community for young mothers, or the grieving, or the like—these can be small communities that foster mutual intimacy in friendship and encourage the heart to grow in God.

Certainly such groups do not replace the particular friendship, with its rich potential for radical shared transformation. Nor do all such groups function at a level of intentionality to encourage the establishment of genuine friendships. Some are designed to fill an immediate and short-lived need. Others are content-oriented, more educational than formational. Nevertheless, small communities, when they foster genuinely mutual and equal love, extend our notions of and the possibility for friendship beyond the classic pairing. They, too, can be fertile ground which produce flower and fruit.

As has been suggested, Jane and Francis thought of their spiritual friendship as embedded in a larger ecclesial reality. God was, in their minds, calling devout souls from many walks of life and strata of society to a more profound intimacy with God's self. This intimate sharing was not only, nor even primarily, for the edification of the individual, but for the whole Christian world. Those whose faith was deepened by devotion were to be like spiritual leaven for the loaf of Christendom. The love of God that was the basis of this calling was catalyzed, compelled and encouraged by the spiritual friendships that were formed between people conscious of that call.

The bishop and the widow-foundress shared an especially intense and rich friendship. But they also enjoyed the companionship of others whom they rightfully could call spiritual friend. For example, we have among Francis' letters the correspondences between himself and Antoine Favre, his fellow countryman and cofounder of the Florimontane Academy (a center of Christian humanist studies), and the Italian Jesuit Antonio Possevino, Francis' teacher, director and friend at the University of Padua. These letters testify to the rich and fruitful exchange between the bishop and these two friends. Possevino was Francis' mentor who continued to inspire and counsel the younger man for years after the latter left the university. It is especially to Possevino that we owe a debt of gratitude for encouraging Francis to take up his pen as part of his spiritual calling.

Antoine Favre shared, not only a birthplace with Francis, but many achievements: the scholarly achievements of the Florimontane, the apostolic work of converting the Protestants, several literary projects, including a legal codex for the duchy of Savoy. He and Francis shared a vision of Christian life and encouraged one another in its pursuit for many years.

Jane, too, fostered God-centered relationships both within her community and with persons outside. We have numerous extant letters to the likes of Jacqueline

Favre, with whom Jane founded the Visitation, as well as letters to her grown children, her brother, and benefactors and friends of the community. In all of these letters Jane shows herself as friend to all. What she, and Francis, envisioned was a community of hearts bound together in mutual, passionate love of God. Like Jesus, whose heart burned with divine desire, so human hearts enflame one another in their shared love.

> Since our Lord, in His goodness, has gathered our hearts into one, allow me, my dearest Sisters, to greet you all, as a community and individually; for this same Lord will not allow me to greet you in any other way. But what a greeting it is! The very one that our great and worthy Father taught us: LIVE JESUS! Yes, my beloved Sisters and daughters, I say the words with intense delight: LIVE JESUS in our memory, in our will, and in all our actions!...strive for that loving union of hearts which brings about a holy peace and the kind of blessing we should desire to have in the house of God and His holy Mother.[5]

Spiritual friendships such as the bishop and the widow cultivated were relationships forged "in the spirit," under the guidance of and in the service of God's animating spirit. No individual friendship could thus be conceived apart from this wider community of friends.

For Reflection

- *Have you experienced friendship in the context of a group setting? What was it like?*

- *What does your parish or congregation offer in terms of group experiences? How might these be established or enriched to encourage spiritual friendship?*

- *How do the particular friendships you share relate to the wider community of the Church?*

- *Hold an imaginary parish meeting in which you invite Jane de Chantal to be present. Tell her about the experience of community within your present parish. Let her advise you.*

For Further Reflection and Discussion

With other writers I can share ideas, but you seem to communicate something deeper. It is as if we met on a deeper level of life on which individuals are not separate beings. In the language familiar to me as a Catholic monk, it is as if we were known to one another in God. This is a very simple and to me obvious expression for something quite normal and ordinary, and I feel no need to apologize for it. I am convinced that you understand me perfectly. It is true that a person always remains a person and utterly separate and apart from every other person. But it is equally true that each person is destined to reach with others an understanding and a unity which transcend individuality, and Russian tradition describes this with a concept we do not fully possess in the West—*sobornost*.[6]—Thomas Merton

Closing Prayer

God, we believe
   that you are a community of three.
Your innermost self

is alive in relationship.

When we live in you
　　we too enter into relationship,
not only with you
　　but with all others who are your friends.

May we savor this truth.
May we delight in the
　　many bonds that tie us,
　　finally, to you.

May we discover
　　the gift of friendship
within the community
　　of your friends.

Notes

[1] *The Gospel in Art by the Peasants of Solentiname*, ed. Philip and Sally Scharper (Maryknoll, N.Y.: Orbis Books, 1984), p. 42.

[2] Francis de Sales and Jane de Chantal, *Letters of Spiritual Direction*, Classics of Western Spirituality Series. Trans. Peronne-Marie Thibert, V.H.M., ed. and intro. Wendy M. Wright and Joseph F. Power, O.S.F.S. (Mahwah, N.J.: Paulist Press, 1988), p. 247.

[3] Ibid., p. 241.

[4] Ibid., p. 261.

[5] Ibid., pp. 239-40.

[6] Letter to Boris Pasternak in *The Courage for Truth: The Letters of Thomas Merton to Writers*, ed. Christine M. Bochen (New York: Farrar, Straus, Giroux, Inc., 1993), pp. 87-88.

DAY SEVEN
The Passion of Friends

Coming Together in the Spirit

> God is love,
> and those who abide in love abide in God,
> and God abides in them....
> There is no fear in love,
> but perfect love casts out fear;... (1 John 4:16, 18,
> NRSV)

God, who is love, sends us love letters. These intimate
missives embolden us to know ourselves as beloved
friends. We dare to recognize our human friendships as
vessels through which we are changed and formed into
persons who more clearly image the God who is love.
Take this thought with you into your retreat today.

Defining Our Thematic Content

If the Scriptures are love letters from God inviting us
to enter more deeply into the relationships that sustain
our deepest lives, we must respond to that invitation.
This brief retreat has introduced us to three people in the
history of the spiritual tradition—Jane de Chantal,
Francis de Sales and Aelred of Rievaulx—who have taken

that invitation seriously. Convinced that the love of God was one with the love of others, and that the two loves were not antithetical, these three taught that human love, especially the love of friends, is a spiritual pathway that could be formative.

Friendship, when its primary content and goal is the cultivation of love and the awakening of the heart to God's loving presence, is a spiritual practice of significance next to none. Our retreat directors have made us aware of love as the foundational dynamic of the world and its careful cultivation as central to our lives. They have alerted us to the fact that friendships require focus, discernment and nurturing. They have taught us that friendships can lead into intensely intimate encounters that challenge our present categories.

Our directors have cautioned us that friendships can take many forms and that they are often best explored within the context of a loving, faith-filled community. In the last day of our retreat, we will turn to the theme of the "passion of friends," to the experience of dying, letting go, absence and empty-handedness that balances the passionate intimacy experienced between those whose love takes the form of friendship.

Again, we turn to Christian tradition for an example of the passion shared by loving friends. In the eighth century, an Anglo-Saxon nun by the name of Lioba, with her fellow missionary Boniface, traveled to Germany to establish the Christian religion in that as yet pagan land. Lioba was not only a soul mate for her friend, but was also his intellectual equal, being a classical scholar of some repute. She was entrusted with the governance of a women's community founded by the bishop on German soil, and so close was their friendship that Boniface granted Lioba permission to pray at his monastery of Fulda, a favor never granted to any other woman before or since that time.

Apparently the two of them experienced their relationship as one that was of an abiding quality, for Boniface made a formal request that when Lioba died she be buried beside him "so that they who had served God during this lifetime with equal sincerity and zeal should await together the day of resurrection." Suffice it to say that the monks of Fulda, scandalized by the thought, did not carry out the request after Boniface's death.

Opening Prayer

Love,
you showed yourself to us
    both as most intimate
    and most absent.

Your love came enfolded in the tender flesh
    of a little child.
    It also came in the torn,
    embattled flesh of the cross.

Teach us to love in both these ways,
    arms tenderly enfolding,
    yet hands empty,
    arms stretched wide.

RETREAT SESSION SEVEN

Any genuine love relationship not only delights and consoles the lovers, it challenges and confronts them. If love stretches the heart, that stretching is not only a joy-filled and energizing expansion, it is also a painful pushing beyond the boundaries within which the heart has heretofore been confined. Our retreat directors knew this well. Aelred has one of his dialogue partners, Walter, articulate the fears of those who would shy away from the intense relationship of friendship on the grounds that it is burdensome and painful to take the part of another human being:

> **Walter:** I almost agree with the opinion of those who say that friendship should be avoided, on the ground that it is a compact full of solicitude and care, not devoid of fear, and even subject to many griefs. For since it is enough and more than enough for anyone to bear his own burden, they say a man acts rashly in so tying himself to others, that he must needs be involved in many cares and afflicted with many evils. Moreover, they think nothing is more difficult than for friendship to abide even to the day of death, while on the other hand it would be quite shameful for a friendship to be formed and then turn into the opposite. Therefore they judge it safer so to love others as to be able to hate them at will, and in so relaxed a manner to hold the reins of friendship that they may be tightened or loosened at will.[1]

Love does indeed ask us not only to enjoy the beloved but to bear the burden and pain that the other bears. It involves not only intimate consolation but dying and desolation as well. Thus the ultimate expression of Love, God's revelation of self, takes the form of a self-emptying death on a cross. Francis de Sales knew this so thoroughly that the last chapter of his book, *Treatise on the Love of God*, which is concerned with divine and human love in all their variations, ends with a meditation entitled "That

Mount Calvary Is the Academy of Love."

> ...Mount Calvary is the mount of lovers. All love
> that takes not its beginning from Our Saviour's
> Passion is frivolous and dangerous. Unhappy is
> death without the love of the Saviour, unhappy is
> love without the death of the Saviour! Love and
> death are so mingled in the Passion of Our Saviour
> that we cannot have the one in our heart without the
> other. Upon Calvary one cannot have life without
> love, nor love without the death of Our Redeemer.
> But, except there, all is either eternal death or
> eternal love: and all Christian wisdom consists in
> choosing rightly....[2]

Just as the passion and cross were necessary to Jesus'
rising, so, too, in spiritual friendships the passion of
intimate union is accompanied by the passion of loss and
letting go. Our retreat directors knew that the love of
friendship is particular in its mutuality and equality. It is
also particular in that it does not mimic any of the other
loves. It is not the filial attachment of a child's love nor
the nurturing solicitude of a parent. Neither is it the
life-conjoining love of spouses or the consummated eros
of lovers. Friendship balances desire and denial, intimacy
and otherness. Its passionate intimacy is tempered by the
recognition of the separateness and autonomy of the
friends.

It is not only in their writings but in the living out of
their actual relationships that our retreat directors are our
mentors in the art of spiritual friendship. We have seen
how Francis and Jane drew closer and transformed each
other's lives over the years. But there came a time when
their intimacy gave way to the shared recognition that to
plunge further into God's love they needed to focus their
relationship differently.

They came to this recognition in 1616. The catalyst
was Jane's annual retreat. She had entered her solitude
knowing that Francis was ill, and she found herself
unable to attend to the prayer theme of her retreat which
was, ironically, detachment. The letters they exchanged
during this retreat have been preserved for us and give us
insight into the process of their gradual detachment from
one another. Just before she retired to her retreat, Jane
had prayed that she not be spared but achieve a perfect
and unconditional surrender to God so that she, like Saint
Paul, could claim "I live, now not I, but Jesus Christ lives
in me." On retreat she found herself distracted from this
goal but preoccupied with Francis' state of health.

> How are you feeling, my poor dear Father? Always
> better by the grace of God? Oh, please, my good
> Saviour, I have been praying for such a long time
> that my Father's precious health be restored....
> Could I remain in my precious solitude a few days
> longer, and continue with my latest meditation? I
> have had a great inclination to quiet my spirit in
> God a bit more. Because, to tell the truth, I have been
> a bit distracted these past days and if your illness
> has not made me anxious, it has grieved me and
> been a distraction. On three separate occasions,
> when it was spoken of to me, I was touched to the
> quick. When I was told that it was dangerous, you
> can imagine my dearest Father, where that led. Oh!
> Lord, help me. May he be blessed.[3]

Francis' response shows that he is aware of the irony that
Jane's pursuit of her deepest prayer is thwarted by her
preoccupation with him. So, taking the reins as her
spiritual guide, he conducts her away from that
preoccupation. Francis deems himself Jane's "wetnurse"
and suggests that the appropriate time for weaning her

from him has arrived.

> My very dear Mother, ...I would like you to continue
> the exercise of denuding yourself and abandoning
> yourself to Our Lord and to me. But, my dear
> mother, I ask you to include some acts on your own
> in the form of ejaculatory prayers that accord with
> the denudation. For example: "I want this, Lord;
> pull, pull firmly from my heart all that clothes it. Oh
> Lord, I do not withhold anything; separate me from
> myself. Oh myself, I leave you forever until
> Monseigneur commands me to take you back."
> These must be asserted gently but firmly.
> Furthermore, my very dear Mother, you must
> not take any kind of nurse but you must leave the
> one who nonetheless still remains and become like a
> poor little pitiful creature completely naked before
> the throne of divine mercy, without ever asking for
> any act or feeling whatsoever for this creature. At
> the same time, you must become indifferent to
> everything that it pleases God to give you, without
> considering if it is I who serve as your nurse.
> Otherwise, if you took a nurse to your own liking
> you would not be going out of yourself but you
> would still have your own way which is, however,
> what you wish to avoid at all costs....
> Write and tell me how you find this lesson. God
> wants to possess me forever. Amen. For I am his
> here and also where I am in you, most perfectly, as
> you know; for we are indivisible except in the
> exercise and practice of renunciation of our whole
> selves to God.[4]

Jane replied the same day, and she celebrates the spiritual
"nakedness" she is experiencing.

> Alas, my only Father, how this precious letter does

me good! Blessed be Him who inspired it; blessed also be my Father's heart for ever and ever!

Certainly, I have a great desire and, it seems to me, a firm resolution to remain in my nakedness, by the grace of God—and I hope that he will help me. I feel that my spirit is utterly free and with I don't know what kind of infinite and profound consolation to see itself in God's hands like this. It is true that all the rest of me remains greatly astonished. But if I do well what you have asked me, my only Father, as no doubt I will with God's help, everything will be better still.

I must tell you this: if I wished to allow it, my heart would seek to reclothe itself with the feelings and expectations that it seems that Our Lord has given it.[5]

This letter evoked a vivid response from the bishop:

Oh Jesus! What a blessing and a consolation to my soul to see my Mother completely naked before God! It has been a long time since I have felt such sweetness while daring to sing the response "Naked I came from my mother's womb and naked I will return. The Lord gives and the Lord takes away. Blessed be the name of the Lord."...

Do not make any effort but, grounded in yesterday's resolution, go, my very dear daughter, and hear and incline your ear: forget all the tribe of your other affections "and your father's house" because "the King" has coveted your nakedness and simplicity. Remain resting there, in a spirit of simple confidence without even looking with attention or any care whatsoever.[6]

For Jane, the surrender to God was complete. The shift, at once subtle and profound, from dependence on Francis to dependence upon God alone signaled a new moment in their relationship. Jane's response to the bishop's letter makes this clear.

> My God! my true Father, how deep the razor has cut! Can I remain in this feeling long? At least our good God, if he so pleases, will hold me firm in my resolutions as I wish. Ah! How your words have given my soul strength! How it consoled and touched me where you wrote, "What blessings and consolations my soul has received to see you utterly naked before God!" Oh! May Jesus grant you to continue to be consoled by this and me to have this happiness!
>
> I am full of hope and courage, very calm and tranquil. Thanks to God, I am not anxious to look and see what I have been divested of. I remain very simple, I see it as though it is very far away, but it does not allow me to come near, for, suddenly, I am turned away. Blessed be Him who has denuded me! May his goodness confirm and strengthen me to do his will. When Our Lord gave me the sweet thought that I sent you on Tuesday—to surrender myself completely to him—alas! I did not think that he would begin by making me put my own hand to the work. May he be blessed in everything and may he wish to strengthen me!...
>
> I close by giving you a thousand good nights and by telling you what has occurred to me. It seems to me that I see the two portions of our spirit as only one abandoned and surrendered together to God. So be it, my very dear Father. May Jesus live and reign for ever! Amen. Don't be in a hurry to get up too soon. I am afraid that the coming feast day will make you do too much. God lead you in everything.[7]

The last letter of the exchange comes from Francis.

Our Lord loves you, my Mother; he wants you to be utterly his own. You no longer have any arms to carry you except his, nor any other breast to lean on except his and his providence. Do not let your eyes look elsewhere and do not rest your spirit anywhere except in him alone. Keep your will so simply united to his in all that it pleases him to do to you, in you, by and for you and in all things outside you, so that nothing ever comes between the two of you. Do not think anymore about the friendship nor the unity that God has created between us, nor of your children, your body, your soul, nor anything whatsoever. For you have given everything to God. "Clothe yourself in Our Crucified Saviour," love him in his suffering, offer up prayers to him. Do not do what you must do because you are inclined toward it any longer but purely because it is God's will.[8]

This glimpse into the dynamic of the passion operative in the widow and the bishop's friendship is unique. Unique not only in that it is a rare piece of personal history preserved, but unparalleled because it emerges out of the specificity of their union shaped, as it was, by the piety of seventeenth-century Catholicism. Clearly, not all spiritual friendships follow such a dramatic path. At the same time, it is fair to say that the dynamics of the love shared by friends is different from the dynamic of the love shared between parents and children, spouses or lovers. Especially in the latter cases, love tends to complete union and the conjoining of lives. While friendship can draw forth the depth of desire from a pair, this is tempered by the recognition that friendship is, in the end, a love that can be possessed only with unclasped hands and outstretched arms.

Even when the pitched dynamics of a male-female

friendship are not operative, friends must be prepared to accept separation on all levels: geographical, physical, emotional and even spiritual. For ultimately the spare spirit of solitude does often pervade the love of friends, leaving the friends free to plunge more joyously into the source of all love, God.

For Reflection

- *In your friendships, where do you discover the passion of the cross at work?*

- *Dialogue with Aelred and his companion Walter, either opposing or defending Walter's opinion that friendship should be avoided because it is full of solicitude and care.*

- *Using language that is appropriate to the twentieth century and true to your own experience, describe the "passion" of friends.*

- *If you had been Francis or Jane, would you have conducted your friendship in the way they did? Explain your response.*

- *Arrange for a conversation with Aelred, Francis and Jane to take place. Present before them a real-life friendship with its particular beauty, difficulties and challenges. How do our retreat directors respond to your presentation?*

For Further Reflection and Discussion

The first hint that anyone is offering us the highest love of all is a terrible shock.... How difficult it is to receive, and to go on receiving from others a love that does not depend on our own attraction.... In such a case to receive is harder and perhaps more blessed than to give.... We are all receiving Charity. There is something in each of us that cannot be naturally loved.... We can be forgiven, and pitied, and loved in spite of it, with Charity; no other way.... Thus God, admitted to the human heart, transforms not only Gift-love but Need-love; not only our Need-love of Him, but our Need-love of one another.[9]—C. S. Lewis

We Are Sent Forth

In a grammar school yearbook from the 1950's, I recently found a rhyme inscribed in pale blue ink:

True friends are like diamonds
precious but rare.
False friends are like autumn leaves
found everywhere.

It was a rather predictable sentiment penned by an acquaintance who inscribed the same rhyme in all her classmates' yearbooks. It is frankly sentimental and generic in the way that commonly circulated wisdom statements are. Yet there is nothing sentimental, predictable or common about genuine spiritual friendships. Challenging, transformative, risky, sustaining, consoling, they are as varied as the friends themselves.

This brief retreat has taken us into the worlds and hearts of three of the great masters of the Christian spiritual tradition. All three directors advocated and cultivated the art of spiritual friendship as part of their journey into the depths of God. All three were convinced that that journey is best undertaken in communion and community with others who also venture onto that path. A vital spiritual life is never predictable or conventional. It engages us at the most profound levels of our being and asks everything of us. It asks us to love courageously and generously.

May you be encouraged to go from this retreat accompanied by the witness and the wisdom of Aelred of Rievaulx, Francis de Sales and Jane de Chantal. May you be prepared to respond as boldly and reflectively as they did to the love of others and the love of God.

Closing Prayer

God,
may we boldly call you friend.
May we boldly call each other friend.
May our friendships make us bold enough
to befriend you.

Notes

[1] *On Spiritual Friendship*, p. 80-81.

[2] *Treatise*, pp. 554-55.

[3] *Bond of Perfection*, pp. 164-165.

[4] Ibid., p. 165-166.

[5] Ibid., p. 166.

[6] Ibid., pp. 166-167.

[7] Ibid., pp. 168-169.

[8] Ibid., p. 170.

[9] C. S. Lewis, *The Four Loves* (New York: Harcourt, Brace, Jovanovich, 1960), pp. 181-183.

Deepening Your Acquaintance

With Francis de Sales and Jane de Chantal

_____ . *Francis de Sales: Finding God Wherever You Are. Selected Spiritual Writings*, ed. and intro. Joseph F. Power, O.S.F.S. New York: New City Press, 1993.

_____ . *Francis de Sales, Jane de Chantal: Letters of Spiritual Direction*, ed. and intro. Wendy M. Wright and Joseph F. Power, O.S.F.S., trans. Péronne Marie Thibert, V.H.M., Classics of Western Spirituality Series. Mahwah, N.J.: Paulist Press, 1988.

de Sales, Francis. *Introduction to the Devout Life*, trans. John K. Ryan. Garden City, N.Y.: Doubleday Image Books, 1982.

Ravier, André. *Francis de Sales: Sage and Saint*, trans. Joseph D. Bowler. San Francisco: Ignatius Press, 1988.

_____ . *Saint Jane de Chantal: Noble Lady, Holy Woman*, trans. Mary Emily Hamilton. San Francisco: Ignatius Press, 1989.

Wright, Wendy M. *Bond of Perfection: Jeanne de Chantal and François de Sales*. New York: Paulist Press, 1985.

_____ . *Francis de Sales: Introduction to the Devout Life and Treatise on the Love of God*. New York: Crossroad, 1993.

For further resources about Jane de Chantal and Francis de Sales, contact De Sales Resource Center, 4421 Lower River Road, Stella Niagara, NY 14144, (716) 754-7376.

With Aelred of Rievaulx

Aelred of Rievaulx. *Aelred of Rievaulx's 'Spiritual Friendship,'* trans. and intro. Mark F. Williams. Scranton, Pa.: University of Scranton Press, 1994.

_____ . *Spiritual Friendship*, Cistercian Fathers Series Five, trans. Mary Eugenia Laker. Washington, D.C.: Cistercian Publications, 1974.

McGuire, Brian Patrick. *Brother and Lover: Aelred of Rievaulx*. New York: Crossroads, 1994.

_____ . *Friendship and Community: The Monastic Experience, 350-1250*. Kalamazoo, Mich.: Cistercian Publications, 1988.

Squire, Aelred. *Aelred of Rievaulx: A Study*. London: SPCK, 1969.

Further studies of Aelred and the Cistercian order to which he belonged are best obtained through Cistercian Publications, WMU Station, Kalamazoo, MI 49008.